THE MUSLIM REVOLT

ROGER HARDY

The Muslim Revolt

A Journey Through Political Islam

Columbia University Press
New York

Columbia University Press
Publishers Since 1893
New York   Chichester, West Sussex
Copyright © Roger Hardy 2010
All rights reserved

Library of Congress Cataloging-in-Publication Data

Hardy, Roger.
  The Muslim revolt : a journey through political Islam / Roger Hardy.
    p. cm.
  Includes bibliographical references and index.
  ISBN 978-0-231-70150-1 (alk. paper)
  1. Islam and politics. 2. Islam and world politics. 3. Islam—21st
  century. 4. Jihad. I. Title.

  BP173.7.H374 2010
  320.917'67—dc22

                    2009049907

∞

Columbia University Press books are printed on permanent
and durable acid-free paper. This book is printed on paper with
recycled content.
Printed in India

c 10 9 8 7 6 5 4 3 2 1

In memory of Alan Gilchrist, a true mentor

CONTENTS

INTRODUCTION

THE LONG WAR

'I have come here,' President Barack Obama declared in Cairo in June 2009, 'to seek a new beginning between the United States and Muslims around the world; one based upon mutual interest and mutual respect.'

To deliver so candid a message so early in his presidency suggested a compelling need to break with the past. The speech implied that the current relationship between the US and Islam was not based (or not sufficiently based) on mutual respect. The status quo was dangerous and unacceptable. In short, something had gone badly wrong and had urgently to be fixed.

The US president told his Egyptian audience, 'America is not—and never will be—at war with Islam.' He promised to withdraw all of his country's troops from Iraq by 2012. He pledged to ban torture and shut down the prison at Guantanamo Bay. He described the situation of the Palestinian people as 'intolerable'. The speech was an attempt to draw a line under the Bush years, when America's standing in the Muslim world had slumped to a new low, and many Muslims had become convinced that, despite its denials, the United States was indeed at war with Islam.

The Cairo speech was widely seen as a welcome statement of intent by a young and popular president who, because of his background, embodied multi–cultural tolerance. In a novel way, the man was the message. But as he himself must have realised, it would take more than eloquence and reassurance to repair such a deeply damaged relationship.

* * *

The crisis in relations between Islam and the West is the most important and the most dangerous issue of our time; it is also the least understood.

Evidence of it is everywhere. We see it each time we glance at the internet or a newspaper or a television screen. Across the world, familiar long-standing disputes rooted in ethnic or national identity—Palestine, Kashmir, Chechnya—have acquired a more pronounced religious colouring. They are seen, by a growing number of their protagonists, as holy wars. At the same time, these older conflicts are fuelling and being fuelled by the newer conflicts of the twenty-first century, the post-9/11 wars in Iraq and Afghanistan which are in turn part of the 'long war'—the radically new and still barely understood global struggle between, on the one side, the US and its allies and, on the other, Al-Qaeda and groups of the Al-Qaeda type. This global struggle—now belatedly recognised as ideological as much as military—has as its epicentre the Afghan-Pakistani border. But there are other fronts, or potential fronts, in Central Asia, in Yemen, in the Horn of Africa and the Maghreb and, alarmingly for the West, in Europe.

These older and newer conflicts are accompanied and aggravated by a third phenomenon. President Obama referred to it in his Cairo speech when he spoke of 'the sweeping change brought by modernity and globalisation' which, he said, had 'led many Muslims to view the West as hostile to the traditions of Islam'. The idea is scarcely new, but it is taking the form of 'culture wars' over the headscarf, over the Danish cartoons, over secular-versus-religious values—controversies which nowadays burn brightly not only in the heartlands of Islam but on its new frontier, the West (and on which the media cheerfully throw fuel).

These conflicts involve states but they are, at root, people's wars. Although each has its own local dynamics, each fertilises the others. The local and the global intermingle. But if evidence of the crisis is everywhere, its causes are hotly contested. Experts explain Muslim militancy by variously invoking the *historical* (a yearning to recapture former glory), the *political* (resistance to Western imperialism and local autocracy), the *economic* (a response to poverty and under-development), the *ideological* (the brainwashing effect of a fierce and reactionary worldview) and the *cultural* (Islam is inherently aggressive, intolerant and anti–Western). This last, although fashionable, seems to me bogus. But the five factors are neither exhaustive nor mutually exclusive.

In the wake of the attack on the Twin Towers on 9/11, I was invited to an unusual dinner in the City of London. A group of businessmen, shocked and perplexed by an event without precedent, had asked two of us who knew something about the Middle East to shed light on what had happened and, more challenging still, what might happen next. The moment was highly charged. This was no ordinary crisis but one which, in Fred Halliday's words, had 'invaded the psyche'.

I took the plunge. For us in the West, the attack had come out of the blue. It was unprovoked. It had no history, no context. (In the heat of the moment, the mayor of New York had declared explanation obscene.) For the perpetrators, on the other hand, it was revenge. It was a counter-attack. It was a reaction to a long history of Western power and Muslim humiliation, and an attempt to reverse that history. The two perceptions of the event were, needless to say, incompatible. As for the future, this was an assault on the West—on what

Al-Qaeda called the 'Crusader-Jewish alliance'—and it was hard to believe that more attacks, on US and perhaps European cities, would not follow.

It was a first attempt to make sense of an act of violence which none of us could fully comprehend. But the occasion convinced me that, for a great many people, Islam and Islamism are equally mystifying, equally threatening. The dinner was the seed of this book.

* * *

'The West is ill at ease with Islam,' a BBC colleague remarked long before 9/11. 'Even communism was more familiar.' Although for most of the second half of the twentieth century communism had been the West's principal enemy, it had come from *within* the Western world and its intellectual tradition. Islam, in contrast, is alien as well as threatening. We fail to understand it, and we are paying a high price for our failure.

To look only at the events of the last few decades—from, say, the Iranian revolution to 9/11 and the London bombings—is to ignore the much deeper roots of the crisis. Groups of the Al-Qaeda type are protagonists in the latest and most destructive phase of a struggle which Muslims have been waging for more than two hundred years. It is a battle on two fronts—against Western domination, rooted in but not confined to the colonial period, and against the failures and disappointments of modernisation, rooted in autocracy and under-development. I call this struggle the Muslim revolt.

As Chapter One describes more fully, the revolt gathered pace at a time when in much of the Muslim world a deep post-independence malaise had set in, existing ideologies were perceived to have failed and the arrival of the new power of the big Middle Eastern oil producers gave Muslims the chance to challenge an unjust world order. This was a new version of the revolt of the South against the North—in Robert Leiken's terse phrase, 'anti–imperialism exalted by revivalism'.[1]

Much of the anger and impatience of the Muslim revolt stems from the fact that Muslims tend to perceive the West and Western modernity—despite their material attractions—as a giant bulldozer crushing all in their path. Western power is seen as an existential threat to the very survival of Islam and Islamic societies. In the political realm, it deprives Muslims of any meaningful autonomy. If their governments are in thrall to the West—or to the World Bank, which amounts to much the same thing—then their independence is a sham. At the same time, globalised Western culture—with its sexual freedoms, its secularism, its rampant consumerism—is seen as inherently inimical to religious values and in particular to the integrity of the family, viewed as the citadel of the faith. (Such fears are, of course, by no means confined to Muslims.)

In the conflicted relationship between Islam and the West, perceptions (which are a kind of reality) play a large part. There is a perceived clash of civilisations, fought out in books and newspapers and on television chat shows, as well as on more conventional battlefields. Although it is by any measure an unequal contest, both sides consider themselves under siege. Muslims feel they are under siege from an aggressive modernity that leaves no corner of the globe untouched. Many in the West—and for that matter secularists and secular governments in the Muslim world—feel themselves besieged by an insurgent Islam which has captured the grass roots and now beats insistently at the gates of power.[2]

Recent developments have heightened such concerns. The new and growing Muslim communities in the West are widely seen as a Trojan horse: the enemy within the gates. What's more, the bombings in New York, Madrid and London—and other thwarted attempts—have intensified the fear that Muslim violence is not confined to the Greater Middle East and that Western cities are vulnerable, too. Mutual demonisation goes hand in hand with mutual paranoia, and the perception of a clash of civilisations gradually hardens into a reality.

* * *

Why another book about political Islam? My hope is that perhaps a journalist may help explain a phenomenon that still seems to madden and perplex both the public and the policy-makers. The form of the book is a journey. Using my travels and encounters as a journalist over the last thirty years, I have tried to create two narratives. The first explores the role of Islam in particular countries or regions—Egypt, Iran, Pakistan, Sudan, Saudi Arabia, Turkey, south-east Asia and Europe. These chapters may seem self-contained, and to some extent they are, but they are links in the chain of a second, overarching narrative which tells the story of Islamism from its origins in the period of European colonialism to the emergence of the global jihadists of today.

What do they have in common, the array of characters that appear in these pages—the Egyptian reformer and the Dutch-Moroccan taxi driver, the Sufi intellectual in Pakistan and the SDGT (specially designated global terrorist) in Saudi Arabia, the Turkish general in Istanbul and the Indonesian schoolgirl singing a Mariah Carey love song? The short and not entirely satisfactory answer is that they are all, in some sense, Muslim. They belong, in a variety of ways, to a world of Islam whose heartland stretches from Mauritania to Mindanao and that comprises some 1.6 billion people—almost a quarter of human-kind. The Western view of Islam tends to be Arab-centred. But although Islam is Arab in origin, most Muslims live *east* of the Middle East. Almost half are in south Asia, home to the four countries with by far the largest Muslim populations—Indonesia, Pakistan, India and Bangladesh. (Predominantly Hindu

India has a Muslim population of 160 million, about twice that of the biggest Arab country, Egypt.)[3]

Those who appear in the pages that follow may be nominal Muslims or passionate believers or somewhere in between. They may support the Muslim revolt or oppose it; they are unlikely to be indifferent to it. Their very diversity is an implicit rebuke to those who insist on seeing Islam and the Muslim world in one-dimensional terms. Muslims are not homogeneous; neither are they uniquely religious or uniquely anti–Western. To write a book of this kind involves making generalisations—attempting to give shape to Muslim beliefs and experiences as I perceive them—but without endorsing the kind of Muslim exceptionalism in which Islam's critics, as well as some of its most ardent adherents, indulge.

Is Islam, in fact, the central defining feature of Muslim-majority societies? This is at least debatable. The late Albert Hourani argued that such societies are shaped by many factors, of which religion is only one. '[T]here is no such thing as "Islamic society",' he wrote some thirty years ago, 'there are societies partly moulded by Islam, but formed also by their position in the physical world, their inherited language and culture, their economic possibilities and the accidents of their political history. Before Islam was they existed, and if Islam has shaped them, they also have shaped it, each in a different way.'[4]

Ali Allawi, in contrast, in a thoughtful and sombre recent book, *The Crisis of Islamic Civilization*, suggests that what defines the character of a Muslim society is precisely the 'spirit of Islam'—the sum of things that make up a Muslim's inner and outer world—and that this shared civilisation is now imperilled by an all-conquering modernity emanating from the West.[5]

Both men would surely have agreed that we should not reduce Muslim societies to one-dimensional caricatures. Nor should we reduce the long and complex relationship between Islam and the West to a mere saga of battles and bigotry. It is a relationship in crisis, but not because a monolithic 'Islam' and an equally monolithic 'West' have been locked in mortal combat since the Middle Ages. The crisis is to some extent coloured by memories of the past but it is essentially modern in origin—indeed modernity, in the sense of a specific Western project we can date to the colonial era, is a crucial catalyst of that crisis. One might argue that in the age of globalisation the terms 'Islam' and 'the West' no longer have much meaning. Certainly they no longer exist as blocs, as they did in medieval times when they confronted one another across the Mediterranean. Each now inhabits the world of the other. I have used both terms nevertheless as necessary shorthand, signifying states and states of mind.

* * *

The writer and broadcaster Hans Keller once remarked that we all suffer from that form of prejudice which we call experience. On this issue perhaps more than most others, a calm objectivity is in short supply. I bring to the table the prejudices (or experience) of a journalist who has been visiting Muslim countries and communities over a period of three and a half decades. I have talked to Muslims—and critics of Islam—of many stripes, read as widely as I can and talked to scholars and other experts who know much more about particular countries and issues than I do. Formal acknowledgements appear at the end of the book, but my debt to all of the above, and to those who accompanied me on the journey, is immense.

1

DREAM OF REVIVAL

'What is Islam?' asks Hasan Hanafi, before giving his own defiant answer. 'It is a revolt against colonialism from outside and oppression from inside; no more, no less.'

Cairo in spring 2002—just six months after the attacks of 9/11—is a good vantage point from which to view the threadbare relations between Islam and the West. I have been visiting the Egyptian capital for almost thirty years, since the October War of 1973. Some of its features are instantly recognisable: the packed throng of humanity (an Egyptian baby is born every twenty-four seconds), the genial confusion of everyday life, as Cairenes cope with noise, traffic, pollution and the price of bread. Of the Egyptian population of some seventy million, sixteen million—close to a quarter—live below the poverty line.

In 1346 the great Muslim traveller Ibn Battuta described Cairo as 'the mother of cities and seat of Pharaoh the tyrant ... whose throngs surge as the waves of the sea, and can scarce be contained in her for all her size and capacity'.[1] Some of the grandeur may have been lost, but the throngs remain much the same.

Yet since my last visit the city has acquired a harder edge. The onrush of modernity is everywhere, in the new flyovers and apartment blocks and the plush hotels and the ubiquitous mobile phones. Politically, there is a sense of malaise. Egyptians are ill at ease with themselves and with the world. Husni

Mubarak, their leader for over two decades and a man viewed in Western capitals as an indispensable ally, is heading into the twilight of his rule. In the wake of 9/11, the threat of the global *jihad* to the West and its Muslim allies is on everyone's minds.

Hasan Hanafi, now in his late sixties, is a professor of philosophy at Cairo University. Educated in Cairo and at the Sorbonne, he has long advocated an Islam of the left—a kind of Islamic liberation theology. He is a prolific talker. Receiving me in the cavernous library of his home, he expounds on Islam and modernity—the 'two lungs' of his body. 'I belong to an Islamic tradition. Islam became a mass culture for the people. No one can do anything without Islam, or against Islam. This is my first lung.' As to the second, he rejects the fashionable options. 'It is very easy to be a fundamentalist, hiding yourself within the umbrella of the old. And it is very easy to be a modern secularist, because the West is there. Both are imitators, both are transferring knowledge, one from the past, one from the present. But the big challenge is: who can breathe from the two lungs at the same time?'[2]

Hanafi is both philosopher and social critic, eloquent in condemning the divisions and inequities of the Muslim world and in emphasising the imperative of social justice. He sees religion as the 'cry of the oppressed'. He believes passionately that decolonisation is not over, but has left unfinished business. Is such a blend of progressive Islam and Third World activism possible? In principle, perhaps; but it is a hard task. Hanafi views his predicament and that of his fellow Muslim reformers with wry humour. 'The Islamists think we are disguised secularists and the secularists think we are disguised Islamists—and the state thinks that we are communist Muslim Brothers'[3] (a reference to the movement whose origins and significance I describe below).

Challenging orthodoxies has got him into trouble. When he was invited to speak at Cairo's prestigious mosque-university of Al-Azhar in 1997, his critics protested, denouncing him as an apostate. After an apparent attempt on his life, he was given round-the-clock police protection. Five years on, he is still under guard. Yet, lonely dissident though he may seem, Hasan Hanafi is heir to a long and rich tradition, a child of the Islamic revival whose roots are firmly embedded in Egyptian soil.

* * *

The story of Islam is one of power, decline and revival. Its founder, Muhammad (570–632), was both prophet and warrior. For the faithful, his historic accomplishment was to receive the divine revelation which was set down in the Qur'an and became the essential framework for Muslim life and Muslim law. But Muhammad established not merely a religion and a code but a community—the model for what the historian Ira Lapidus calls a 'worldwide family of societies'.[4]

The Prophet transformed the warring tribes of Arabia into a federation under his control. It was as a political and military force that the Arabians set out, under the banner of Islam, on the road of conquest. Under the caliphs who succeeded Muhammad, Islam took on two empires—the Byzantine and the Sasanian—and from them shaped its own. Little more than a century after the Prophet's death, that empire stretched from Spain to Samarkand. The Muslims established centres of power and culture in Damascus and Baghdad and eventually in Cairo, Fez and beyond.

Contrary to popular belief, the Arabs did not as a rule impose Islam at the point of a sword. Their language, Arabic, spread fairly slowly and their religion more slowly still. It was not until the period between the tenth century and the thirteenth that the mass of Middle Eastern peoples were converted to Islam, and then largely for practical purposes: the empire worked better as a Muslim than as a purely Arab enterprise.

This first empire produced a remarkable civilisation—reflected in the Dome of the Rock in Jerusalem and the gardens and courtyard of the Alhambra in Muslim Spain—but it was also wracked by dissension and civil war. The most serious rift occurred a quarter of a century after the Prophet's death and reflected disagreement over who should succeed him as leader of the Muslim community: this was the split between the Sunni and Shi'ite branches of Islam.

What were Islam's defining features? It was, above all, a religion of justice. It urged the faithful to 'command right and forbid wrong'—which meant they had a duty to correct the behaviour of other Muslims as well as to follow the right path themselves. While some sought to interpret rightful behaviour as voluntary—mindful of the Qur'anic phrase 'there is no compulsion in religion'—others interpreted the injunction in a more authoritarian spirit. The legacy of these alternative views is still alive today.[5]

In its heyday, Islam was not just a faith and a civilisation. It was a superpower and, as such, posed both a military and an ideological challenge to European Christendom. Christians saw Islam as the 'enemy on the frontier'.[6] 'The existence of Islam,' writes the historian R. W. Southern, 'was the most far-reaching problem in medieval Christendom.' The fact that it was immensely successful and would not succumb to either conquest or conversion made the Christians profoundly uneasy.[7]

The two sides confronted one another across the Mediterranean in an ebb and flow of power. During the Crusades, the Christians for a time displaced the Muslims from Jerusalem and its holy places. Then they in turn were expelled almost a century later by the great Muslim warrior Saladin and his army. The Crusades have become an enduring symbol of hostility between Islam and the West. The historian Thomas Asbridge calls the First Crusade, launched by Pope Urban II in 1095, a watershed: 'This was not the first war between Christians and Muslims, but it was the conflict that set these two religions on a course towards deep-seated animosity and enduring enmity. Between 1000 and 1300 CE Catholic Europe and Islam went from being occasional combatants to avowed and entrenched opponents.'[8]

Europe's encounter with Islam during the First Crusade did not bring about knowledge but, on the contrary, what Southern calls 'the ignorance of the triumphant imagination'. The Crusaders saw Islam as a dark parody of Christianity and the Prophet as the anti–Christ: a magician, a sensualist and a deceiver. This depth of ignorance began to recede as scholars and travellers acquired a more detailed and accurate understanding of Islam and the East. Nevertheless the Crusades became 'imagined history', embedded in Christian and Muslim folk memory. When the French army took Damascus in 1920, their commander went to Saladin's tomb and declared, '*Nous revoilà, Saladin*' (We're back, Saladin). In the 1950s and 1960s many Arabs viewed the popular Egyptian leader Gamal Abdel-Nasser as a new Saladin who would liberate Jerusalem from the new Crusaders (the Israelis). Contemporary jihadists refer to their principal enemies not as the US and Israel but as the 'Crusader-Jewish alliance'. George Bush, when he was president, was dubbed the Crusader-in-chief and Condoleezza Rice, his secretary of state, the 'Crusader hag'. For the jihadists, as for some Christian fundamentalists, the 'clash of civilisations' is very real: it began with the early confrontation between Islam and Christendom and will continue until the end of days.

Islam's moment in history lasted roughly a thousand years. After the decline of the first Arab-Islamic empire, the geographical focus shifted. Between 1400 and 1600 Muslim power became consolidated into three great dynasties—Turkish (Ottoman), Persian (Safavid) and Indian (Mughal). Emblems of their glory remain in the mosques built for Suleiman the Magnificent in Istanbul, in the ornate *madrasas* (seminaries) of Isfahan and in that masterpiece of Mughal culture, the Taj Mahal.

Only after 1700 did the balance of power between Islam and the West begin to shift decisively in the West's favour. The shock, when it came, was profound. Islam had been 'programmed for victory'.[9] Dominance was the natural order of things. Its loss was hard to bear.

* * *

On 19 May 1798 a young Napoleon Bonaparte, not yet thirty, set sail for Egypt. He brought with him 400 ships and over 50,000 soldiers, sailors and marines. He expressed his strategic purpose succinctly: 'To ruin England we must make ourselves masters of Egypt.' The French forces reached Alexandria on 1 July and from there marched on Cairo, where they defeated the country's Mamluk rulers at the Battle of the Pyramids. It was the first major incursion of a European power into the heart of the Muslim world since the Crusades. For the Egyptian historian Abdel-Rahman al-Jabarti, who witnessed it, it signified 'the beginning of the reversal of the natural order and the corruption or destruction of all things'. In his first proclamation, issued in Arabic, Napoleon assured the Egyptians that 'the French are true Muslims' and that they 'worship God far more than the Mamluks do, and respect the Prophet and the glorious Qur'an'.[10] (Al-Jabarti considered the Frenchman's Arabic atrocious.)

Napoleon brought with him scientists as well as soldiers, and an attitude of mind. 'The French occupation of Egypt in

1798 was not only an incident in the [Anglo-French] revolutionary wars, it was a movement of the imagination. Bonaparte had read the Comte de Volney's *Voyage en Egypte et en Syrie* and other writings about Egypt, and they helped to shape his actions there: he was conscious of forty centuries looking down on him and his soldiers: he thought of himself as coming to bring back life to a lifeless world, and the scholars and scientists who went with him carried out the first systematic appropriation of an oriental society and culture.'[11]

The civilising mission was part and parcel of Napoleon's colonial purpose. Accompanying his expedition were 151 *savants*—scientists, engineers and artists who proceeded to analyse Egypt in extraordinary detail. They surveyed the whole country and made new maps. They studied and drew its flora and fauna. They measured the Sphinx. They looked for ways to purify the waters of the Nile. They studied how the Egyptians baked bread. They dissected bird mummies. One scientist produced an optical explanation for the desert mirage. The results of these labours were brought together in the *Description de l'Egypte*, published in twenty-three volumes (thirteen of engravings and ten of text, each page a metre square) between 1809 and 1828. Napoleon did not live to see its completion.

For the Muslims of Egypt, the colonial encounter provoked a mixture of emotions. One was puzzlement. Al-Jabarti was struck by the invaders' odd behaviour, in particular their 'slavery to women'. When he visited the French scientists, they introduced him to such novelties as electricity. As Egyptians observed the foreigners' new-fangled gadgets of science and war, they could not fail to be conscious of the gap in knowledge and power between themselves and the Europeans. At the same time there could be no doubt that this was a mission of conquest, not merely one of scientific enquiry. There was fierce resistance to attempts by the colonial invaders to administer and transform the country. In October 1798, after two days of rioting, French forces shelled Cairo and sacked the famous mosque-university of Al-Azhar. Some 3,000 Egyptians lost their lives. During a subsequent revolt, in 1801, the French lost control of the city for a full five weeks.[12]

The occupation was short-lived. In September 1801, little more than three years after they had arrived, Napoleon's generals surrendered to the British. (Bonaparte himself had already escaped back to France.) One result of the episode was that Egyptians lost faith in their Mamluk rulers, and in 1805 the *ulama* (religious scholars) appealed to an up-and-coming Turkish soldier from Macedonia to take over the governing of the country. This was Muhammad Ali (1769–1849), who ruled Egypt for more than forty years in what proved to be a formative period in its emergence as a modern state. He modernised the army, reformed the economy, created a civil service and introduced the train, the telegraph and the printing-press.

But Muhammad Ali's successors lacked his drive and ability, and continuing Anglo-French rivalry ensured that European intervention was far from over. The country became hopelessly indebted to its foreign creditors. The construction of the Suez Canal, inaugurated in 1869, was in one sense a mark of modernity, but it came at a cost of 100,000 Egyptian lives. Rather than symbolising the country's growing strength and autonomy, it underlined its abject dependence on foreign powers. From the 1880s, that meant Britain, whose occupation of the country was to last until 1954.

An expansionist Europe, with its science, technology and ideas, represented a new set of challenges to a weak Muslim world. Among the educated, radical and subversive new political concepts began to circulate, such as parliamentary democracy, the separation of religion and state and the emancipation of women. The question of the day was how to respond to Western power and Western modernity. Broadly speaking, there were three possible options: acceptance, rejection or synthesis. A small but growing secular élite embraced Westernisation even while chafing under the colonial yoke. The goal of this élite was to replace colonial rule with a form of self-government consciously modelled on the modern liberal European nation-state. Traditionalist Muslims, on the other hand, saw Westernisation as going hand in hand with secularisation and therefore as an existential threat to the faith and the faithful.

The third and hardest option was synthesis—in Hasan Hanafi's phrase, breathing with both lungs at the same time. This was the option pursued by such early Egyptian reformers as Muhammad Abduh (1849–1905), who declared it his life's work 'to return, in the acquisition of religious knowledge, to its first sources, and to weigh them in the scale of human reason ... and to prove that, seen in this light, religion must be accounted a friend of science'.[13]

Like other liberals, Abduh was strongly influenced by European culture and learning but firmly opposed to European colonialism. At a meeting with a British official he is reported to have declared: 'We Egyptians of the Liberal Party believed once in English liberalism and English sympathy; but we believe no longer, for facts are stronger than words. Your liberalness we see plainly is only for yourselves, and your sympathy with us is that of the wolf for the lamb which he designs to eat.'[14]

Abduh had studied at Cairo's pre-eminent seat of Muslim learning, Al-Azhar, and was dismayed at its stultifying atmosphere. This convinced him that education was the key to the revival of Islam and the modernisation of Egypt. His relationship with the authorities, however, was strained by his nationalist sympathies. He was forced into exile and eventually went to Paris to join another well-known reformer, his friend Jamal al-Din al-Afghani. On his return he became a judge and in 1899 Egypt's Grand Mufti, a position from which he was able to promote his ideas with greater authority. His views were, for their time, remarkably progressive. He advocated equal rights for women, opposed polygamy and did not believe the veiling of women should be obligatory.[15]

Central to his beliefs was the conviction that if Muslims were to engage with modernity while remaining true to their faith they must revive and practise *ijtihad*, the exercise of independent reasoning. Two of the key principles of classical Islamic thought were *ijtihad* and *taqlid* (imitation). Abduh believed passionately that Muslims needed 'to be liberated from the shackles of *taqlid*'. He blamed the tendency for blind imitation on the conservative *ulama*, who for their part did their utmost to resist his reformist ideas.

This view of the vital importance of *ijtihad* is shared by Abduh's heirs, including Hasan Hanafi. 'We lost our pluralism, our liberalism, a thousand years ago,' he told me, when the influential Muslim philosopher Al-Ghazali set the seal on a rigid orthodoxy suspicious of innovative thought. 'When Al-Ghazali came—it was the beginning of the Crusades—he felt that pluralism, enlightenment, may be risky once you begin to face the external enemy. Then he wanted to make a strong state, he wanted to make one school in dogma, one school in law. And he even discredited our democracy, legitimising taking power by force—the *coup d'état*—because the state needs a strongman. Till now we are suffering from this.'

In a much-debated phrase, Al-Ghazali and the religious scholars of his day 'closed the gates' of *ijtihad*. Muslim reformers from Abduh to Hanafi have made it their business to pry them open.

But there was an inherent weakness in Abduh's position. 'The presumed values of modernity (*à la européene*) were implicitly taken as the standard against which Islam was to be measured.'[16] Traditional Islamic concepts had to be identified with the dominant ideas of modern Europe. Hence *maslaha* (the common good) became utility; *shura* (consultation) parliamentary democracy; *ijma* (consensus) public opinion. But some of his critics were not persuaded by this; indeed they saw its inherent danger. Although Abduh 'had intended to build a wall against secularism, he had in fact provided an easy bridge by which it could capture one position after another'.[17]

Abduh's influence on later reformers was significant, and many acknowledged their intellectual debt to him. Politically, however, the liberals made little headway. Synthesis of the kind they advocated was suspect. Most Egyptians chose rejection of the West, expressed in the language of an essentially secular nationalism. The British failure to grasp that Egyptian nationalism was an authentic force, with wide popular appeal, was embodied in the autocratic and unyielding figure of Sir Evelyn Baring (later to become Lord Cromer), who governed the country from 1883 until 1907. This was the period of the 'veiled protectorate', when, in the words of a distinguished Egyptian historian, Baring ruled 'from behind a façade of Egyptian ministers who had little authority, and were rubber stamps for their British manipulators'.[18]

Strategically, Egypt's role was to guard the route to British-ruled India; economically, to provide a constant supply of cotton for the mills of Lancashire. Despite the promises of successive officials that British rule was temporary, 'Baring believed that "subject races" were totally incapable of self-government, that in fact they did not really want or need self-government, and that what they really needed was a "full belly" policy which fed the population, kept it quiescent and allowed the élite to make money and so co-operate with the occupying power.'[19] He regarded Islam as reactionary and incapable of change, famously declaring, 'Islam reformed is Islam no longer.'

Opposition to colonial rule gathered pace after the First World War and was led by Saad Zaghloul (1859–1927) and his nationalist Wafd Party. By the early twentieth century, most Muslim states were under some form of foreign rule. Britain and France controlled much of the Middle East, the Italians occupied Libya, Tsarist Russia dominated Muslim Central Asia and the Dutch governed what was to become Indonesia. Everywhere the European presence provoked a nationalist response. But in some places—including Egypt from the late 1920s—the nationalists began to face an increasingly forceful rival in the form of movements which expressed opposition to foreign rule in the language of Islam.

* * *

Mamoun Hudeibi is a big, gruff man in his mid-seventies. A former judge, he is a seasoned political survivor. When I visit him, in the spring of 1995, he is the deputy leader of the Muslim Brotherhood, the oldest and largest Islamic political movement and the grandparent of the more radical groups of today, including their most violent offshoot, Al-Qaeda.[20]

Sitting in a nondescript office in Cairo, Hudeibi reminisces in deep, fruity Arabic about the movement's founding father, his friend and mentor Hasan al-Banna (1906–49). Al-Banna was a modest man, he says, but had real charisma. His origins were humble. He was born in a provincial town in the Nile delta—where his father was a local *imam* who repaired watches in his spare time—and went on to become a school-teacher in Ismailiya, on the Suez Canal. Strongly influenced by the daily reality of British rule, he rejected both colonialism and secular nationalism. In 1928, at the age of only twenty-two, Al-Banna created the Society of Muslim Brothers—better known as the Muslim Brotherhood—out of the conviction that Egypt had to be Islamised, or re-Islamised, to regain its strength and true identity. His dream was of the revival of Muslim power and civilisation, which had to be predicated on the rekindling of Islamic belief and consciousness at the grass roots. Loyalty to the *umma* (the worldwide community of Muslims) superseded love of nation-state. The Brotherhood stood for a kind of Muslim patriotism, as well as a belief in the solidarity of the *umma*. It espoused social justice based not on class struggle, as the socialists advocated, but on equality under Islam. It was a social movement rather than a political party.

Al-Banna was the father of Islamism—the notion that Islam was not just a religion and a way of life but an all-encompassing political and social ideology, a twentieth-century 'ism'. From the start, Islamism had both an internal and an external dimension. Its purpose was to bring Muslims back to the fold, thereby recreating a community modelled on that of the Prophet in the city of Medina in seventh-century Arabia. At the same time it was a kind of liberation movement, committed to freeing Muslims from non-Muslim rule. In the colonial era this was of paramount importance. It meant liberating Egypt and all other Muslim lands from foreign occupation, and in particular helping the Arabs of Palestine resist British rule and Zionist colonisation. In Al-Banna's mind, the internal and external dimensions were linked. 'Eject imperialism from your souls,' he declared, 'and it will leave your lands.'

I ask Hudeibi what sort of man Al-Banna was. 'He was a very modest man, but very perceptive. He was a captivating speaker. Above all, his knowledge of the principles and concepts of Islam was enormous. He travelled tirelessly round the country from Aswan [in the south] to Alexandria [in the north]—and once he met someone he'd never forget them.

Even if they met again ten or twenty years later, he'd remember the man's name and ask after his wife and children.'

Al-Banna's mission, says Hudeibi, was 'to work towards reviving the Muslim nation and to open people's eyes to the reality of religion, which had become remote from many of the common people, and indeed from many intellectuals'. Al-Banna saw the overriding challenge as the pervasive secularising influence of the West. After leaving his small home town in the 1920s to study in Cairo, he wrote, in almost despairing tones, of what he perceived as a vital but unequal struggle: 'I saw the social life of the beloved Egyptian people, oscillating between her dear and precious Islam which she had inherited, defended, lived with during fourteen centuries, and this severe Western invasion which was armed and equipped with all [the] destructive influences of money, wealth, prestige, ostentation, power and means of propaganda.'[21]

To counter this overwhelming Western tide, Al-Banna turned the Brotherhood into a formidable grass-roots organisation. A brilliant organiser—Hasan Hanafi calls him the Marx and Lenin of the Islamic movement—he recruited young men of the lower and middle classes (in other words, from outside the traditional élite) and built up a substantial membership, a youth wing and eventually a clandestine armed militia. By 1944 the Brotherhood had over a thousand branches in Egypt. By the time of Al-Banna's death five years later, it probably had around half a million active members and branches in several parts of the Middle East.

After the Second World War the movement took part in the increasingly violent campaign waged by Egyptians against the British occupation. In December 1948 one of its members assassinated the prime minister. A few weeks later, in retaliation, members of the secret police approached Al-Banna in Cairo one evening as he was getting into a taxi and shot him dead.

It was a significant blow to the organisation, but did not entirely snuff out its hopes. In 1952 the British-backed monarchy was overthrown in a coup by army officers, some of whom were sympathetic to the Brotherhood. For a moment it seemed possible the two groups might share power. But Egypt's new leader, Gamal Abdel-Nasser, soon became suspicious that the movement was out to undermine him. In 1954, after one of its members tried to assassinate him at a public meeting, he outlawed the Brotherhood, hanged six of its members and sent a thousand more to prison camps.

Al-Banna had done something altogether new: he had created a modern, organised social movement very different from the traditional patronage-based parties of the time. That he did not achieve more was due in part to his death at the age of only forty-two and in part to the potency of the rival force of nationalism. The Islamists had given birth to a new movement, but their moment had not yet arrived. The independence struggles of the Muslim Third World were fought and won under the banner of nationalism, and occasionally the red flag of socialism, rather than the green banner of Islam. Religion remained largely relegated to the sidelines.

Hasan Hanafi, not yet twenty at the time of the Nasserist coup, was swept up in the tide of nationalist fervour. Like countless others who were committed to the anti–colonial struggle, he was convinced an important page had been turned in the history of his country and of the Arabs as a whole. But he had already begun to move, in his own words, from 'national consciousness' to 'religious consciousness'. In the early 1950s he joined the Muslim Brotherhood, convinced it was necessary to combine a commitment to Islam with wholehearted support for the project of national liberation. Even then, his individualism stood out: some of the Brothers disapproved of the fact that he played the violin and liked Western

23

music. Nevertheless he was intellectually a committed Islamist, inspired by the writings of Al-Banna and, like many young Egyptians, captivated by the brilliant, brooding, controversial figure who succeeded him as the ideologue of the Islamist movement.[22]

* * *

Radical Islamism was born in Nasser's jails. Its champion and first martyr was Sayyid Qutb (1906–66). Qutb was a bureaucrat who worked for sixteen years for the Egyptian Ministry of Education, in his spare time writing short stories, poems and literary criticism. His life might have remained utterly conventional but for two events. In 1948 the ministry sent him on a fact-finding mission to the United States, whose materialism, sexual permissiveness and racism he found deeply shocking. On his return home he joined the Muslim Brotherhood and, like other Islamists, welcomed Nasser's seizure of power. The shock and sense of betrayal was all the greater when the new Egyptian ruler turned on them. Qutb was among those arrested in 1954, and it was during his ten years in prison that he produced his seminal work *Milestones*, published in 1964. In its angry denunciation of Nasserism as a symptom of an impious world order, it was a product of his bitter disenchantment with the post-colonial world. If Harry Truman's America had made him, in some sense, a born-again Muslim, incarceration in Nasser's prison camps—where he suffered continuous ill health and brutal torture—transformed him into an ardent revolutionary.

Milestones is a rallying-cry. Capitalism and socialism are bankrupt, Qutb declares. 'Now, at this most critical of times, when turmoil and confusion reign, it is the turn of Islam.' But in facing this critical situation, Muslims are a position of abject weakness. They and their rulers are no better than infidels living in a state of *jahiliyya*—the Dark Ages of pre-Islamic Arabia. A Muslim vanguard must combat *jahiliyya* using the weapon of *jihad*. The rulers must be overthrown, if need be by force.[23]

Qutb views the West in two distinct ways. He admires 'Europe's genius [which] created its marvellous works in science, culture, law and material production, due to which mankind has progressed to great heights of creativity and material comfort'. These achievements are all the more painful for Muslims to behold because 'what we call the "world of Islam" is completely devoid of all this beauty'. But despite its technological and material development, the West has lost its moral compass: 'The leadership of mankind by Western man is now on the decline, not because Western culture has become poor materially or because its economic and military power has become weak. The period of the Western system has come to an end primarily because it is deprived of those life-giving values which enabled it to be the leader of mankind.'[24]

In urging Muslims to fill this moral void, *Milestones* has an urgency and uncompromising militancy which for its readers was altogether new: 'Setting up the kingdom of God on earth, and eliminating the kingdom of man, means taking power from the hands of its human usurpers and restoring it to God alone … and [establishing] the supremacy of the Shari'a [Islamic law] alone and the repeal of all man-made laws … This general call to liberate mankind on earth from all power that is not the power of God … [is] not a theoretical, philosophical or passive one … it [is] a dynamic, active, positive call.'[25]

Qutb's revolutionary message was a significant departure from traditional Brotherhood thinking. Hitherto the enemy had been colonialism. Now, in addition to the infidel West, it was the Muslim régimes—epitomised by Nasser's shabby dictatorship—which Qutb had at a stroke excommunicated.

Nasser himself was not slow to realise the implications of this incendiary message. In 1966, after a show trial, Qutb was hanged for treason.

* * *

What, then, is the essence of the Muslim revolt? A distinguished scholar of Islam wrote half a century ago: 'The fundamental malaise of modern Islam is a sense that something has gone wrong with Islamic history. The fundamental problem of modern Muslims is how to rehabilitate that history: to set it going again in full vigour, so that Islamic society may once again flourish as a divinely guided society should and must.'[26]

Islam had moved along a path from power to decline to revival—or rather the dream of revival, since the dream had yet to be realised. The Muslims' phenomenal early success had been reversed, and this had to be explained as well as remedied. The simplest explanation was that they had lost God's favour: they were no longer behaving as the Prophet and the Qur'an had enjoined, and their back-sliding and disunity had opened the way for Western dominance. This was all the more dangerous because the West was not just rapacious; its moral heart was hollow. Physical conquest and occupation were merely the prelude to cultural corruption—and while conquerors came and went, their corrupting influence endured. The answer was moral rearmament.

Islamism represented a double revolt: against an *imposed* modernity (associated with colonialism) and a *failed* modernity (associated with the post-colonial régimes). Did this mean the Islamists rejected modernity *per se*? On this there was a spectrum of views. Radical rejectionists, such as the followers of Qutb, presented the contest between the West and Islam as a zero-sum game. For them, there could be no compromise with *jahiliyya*: it was a dragon that had to be slain. But, as we have seen, even Qutb found things to admire among the West's material accomplishments. The answer was to create an Islamic modernity—but just what this meant, and how it was to be achieved, was far from clear. It seemed to mean, in practice, picking and choosing, appropriating from the West what was useful and as far as possible value-free, and rejecting what was not. The Islamist impulse was strong but it was not articulated into anything that could be called a programme.

The new movement of 'political Islam', born in Egypt and now spreading through the Muslim *umma*, was from the start contested, and not just by governments. Nationalist and socialist intellectuals considered it primitive and reactionary, an attempt to weaken the nationalist project by invoking religion. Traditionalist Muslims, on the other hand, accused Al-Banna and his followers of trying to hijack the faith for political ends. For them, Islam was about personal and communal piety; the notion that it was an all-embracing political ideology was a grotesque distortion whose effect would be to set Muslim against Muslim—the grave sin of *fitna*. Many traditionalists held that rulers should be tolerated as long as they allowed the faithful to perform their prayers. Tyranny was preferable to disorder—a view the Islamists condemned as abject capitulation to un-Islamic rule.

After Qutb's death, the movement split. The mainstream leadership—under Mamoun Hudeibi's father, Hasan—distanced itself from Qutb's revolutionary creed and sought to avoid violent confrontation with the government. But accusations of links to violence continued to dog the movement. Had not Al-Banna's secret military wing launched a series of assassination attempts directed at the British and politicians tied to them? Had the Brotherhood really broken with its past?

Mamoun Hudeibi was distinctly touchy when I broached the subject. 'These false accusations are made by those in power to combat the Muslim Brotherhood and the preaching of Islam. When a country is occupied, as Egypt was by the British and Palestine by the Zionists, acts of violence against the occupation forces can't be called terrorism. Later on, when mistakes were made, when some individual acted without the knowledge of the group, we admitted there were mistakes and condemned them. But the authorities have tried to exploit such mistakes, to justify their stance against us.'[27]

While the Brotherhood's leaders made survival their priority, a largely clandestine radical wing of the movement sought to keep alive the flame of Qutbism, which over time became one of the sources of inspiration for Al-Qaeda and the radical jihadists.

***

Suppressed by Nasser in the 1950s and 1960s, Islamism survived to experience a second coming. The 'return of Islam' is sometimes dated to the Egyptian ruler's crushing defeat by Israel in the June War of 1967. The latter represented a crisis of conscience for Arabism, the essentially secular doctrine of pan-Arab nationalism that Nasser had championed, and was a moment of painful collective self-doubt. The Iraqi poet Abdul-Wahab al-Bayati captured the mood in a lacerating poem called 'Lament for the June Sun'.[28]

> We are pounded in the café of the East
> War of words
> Wooden swords
> Lies and horsemen of the air.
> We did not kill a camel or a crow:
> We did not try the game of death:
> We did not play with knights or even pawns:
> Our employment trivia
> As we slew each other to the final crumb ...

Arabism's failure to live up to its promise represented Islamism's moment of opportunity. Other factors worked in its favour: one was the new oil wealth of the 1970s enjoyed by the Arab states of the Gulf and North Africa, which seemed to offer Muslims the chance to challenge what they saw as the severe imbalance in the world order; another was the social dislocation associated with rapid modernisation. The population of the Arab states had risen from fifty-five million in 1930 to ninety million in 1960; by the early 1980s it totalled 200 million.

A form of post-independence disenchantment set in. Nationalist leaders had promised their people dignity and development, yet they were increasingly unable to meet their citizens' most basic needs. The new governing élites came to be seen as corrupt and authoritarian, inhabiting a secular world of Western-style consumption far removed from the poverty and piety of the masses. 'The poor, driven to the limit of famine or wretched subsistence [wrote the French scholar Maxime Rodinson], direct their anger and recrimination against the privileges of the rich and powerful—their ties with foreigners, their loose morality and their scorn of Muslim injunctions, the most obvious signs of which are the consumption of alcohol, familiarity between the sexes, and gambling. For them, as Robespierre put it so well, atheism is aristocratic.'[29]

Beginning in the 1970s, an Islamic revival swept through the Muslim world which acquired new force with the Iranian revolution of 1979. Everywhere its trump card was authenticity: Western ideologies—nationalism, liberalism, socialism, Marxism—had been tried and found wanting. Islamism, on the other hand, was home-grown, rooted in Muslim soil. For anyone who visited Egypt at the time, the pace and scope of 'Islamisation' was remarkable. The most obvious external signs—as elsewhere in the Muslim world—were that more young women wore the *hijab*, or headscarf, and more young men sported beards. At the same time new mosques were being built and there was a dramatic expansion of Muslim civil-society organisations of every type, as well as an abundance of Islamic magazines, pamphlets and cassettes.

Anwar Sadat, who succeeded Nasser after his death in 1970, tacitly encouraged Islamisation as part of a broader de-Nasserisation campaign and as an attempt to weaken the political left. This included a realignment of the country towards the West and away from the Soviet Union.

The Islamists seized their opportunity to re-emerge and campuses became the arena for clashes between them and the leftists. The clandestine groups, radical offshoots of the Brotherhood who were inspired by Qutb, resorted to violence against the state. In 1981 the Jihad group, gunned down Sadat—the hated Pharaoh who had signed a peace treaty with Israel—at a military parade.

Under Sadat's successor, Husni Mubarak, the authorities fought a brutal war in the 1990s against two violent groups, Jihad and Gamaa al-Islamiya. They were suppressed, but at a cost of more than a thousand lives. At the same time, the Brotherhood attempted to fend off the charge that it was secretly in league with the militants and that its outward show of pragmatism was merely a smokescreen to hide its desire to overthrow the system. Despite intermittent and often harsh repression, it survived as the country's main opposition group.

One of those swept up in the wave of arrests that followed Sadat's assassination was Ayman al-Zawahiri, a thirty-year-old physician and radical Islamist who represents an important link between Qutbism and Al-Qaeda. Born in 1951 to a well-to-do family in Cairo, as a young man Zawahiri had gravitated towards Islamist politics. His uncle was a close friend of Qutb, visiting him in prison right up to his death, and Zawahiri clearly revered the author of *Milestones* as both ideologue and role model. In 1980 Zawahiri visited Peshawar, in Pakistan, and treated victims of the Afghan war against Soviet occupation—which, from then on, he saw as the *cause célèbre* of the global Islamist struggle.

After his arrest as a member of the Jihad group, Zawahiri claimed to know nothing of the plot to kill Sadat. This did not spare him from being tortured and forced to betray his comrades, which induced in him a mixture of anger and guilt which seems to have endured long afterwards, contributing to an intense and embittered radicalisation. He wrote later of the electric-shock treatment, sexual humiliation and use of 'wild dogs' routinely meted out to Islamists in Egyptian jails.

Released in 1985, Zawahiri left Egypt for Saudi Arabia, where he probably met Osama bin Laden for the first time. The alliance between the radicalised and politically seasoned Egyptian and the wealthy young Saudi became the bedrock of the phenomenon we now know as Al-Qaeda.[30]

* * *

The lift was broken, so I climbed five flights of stairs, past a bored-looking security guard, to reach the Cairo apartment of Muhammad Said al-Ashmawi. It was like an overcrowded *bric-à-brac* shop. Sitting surrounded by clocks, statues and piles of books, Ashmawi told me of his confrontation with Islamism.

Ashmawi was at the time seventy and a well-known writer and former judge. In 1987 he had published an outspoken book which had attacked one of the Islamists' core ideas—that the basis of legislation should be the Shari'a, the holy law of Islam. 'I said the Qur'an is not a legal book,' he told me. 'It is mainly a book for the ethical code and for the faith. And once we are putting a definition to the word Shari'a, we will realise

31

that ninety per cent of what we call Shari'a is actually human, not divine.' The book—called *Al-Islam al-Siyasi* (Political Islam)—argued that the call for an Islamic state governed by the Shari'a was a mere political slogan—'a pretext for self-seeking or a springboard to power'. In short, Islamism posed a danger to Islam and to Egypt.[31]

There was a furious response. Conservatives, including the Sheikh of Al-Azhar, were incensed. Ashmawi was denounced as an apostate and the authorities put a round-the-clock guard on his apartment. His predicament was not unique. A string of similar cases—involving, among others, Hasan Hanafi and the scholar Nasser Abu-Zeid—suggest that, in a country once seen as a beacon of modernism in the Muslim world, free-thinking intellectuals nowadays run considerable risks. Abu-Zeid's offence was to apply modern methods of textual analysis to the Qur'an. He too was denounced as an apostate and taken to court. The law suit was initially rejected, then, when his opponents appealed, accepted. To the consternation of Egyptian liberals, Abu-Zeid was declared an apostate and, as such, his wife was instructed to divorce him. In 1995 they fled to the Netherlands.[32]

* * *

Egypt's role in the Muslim revolt has been crucial. Muhammad Abduh, Hasan al-Banna, Sayyid Qutb, Hasan Hanafi and countless others have all in their different ways struggled to find answers to the question that has haunted Muslims for more than two centuries: how to revive and reinvigorate Islam in a world dominated by Western power, technology and culture?

There are profound differences between the Islamic modernism of Abduh, the populist revivalism of Al-Banna and the revolutionary jihadism of Qutb and Zawahiri. Yet all are part of an Islamic revival which is all too often viewed in one-dimensional terms. Violent rejection of a global *jahili* culture is only one strand within a rich tapestry. The Islamic revival is, at its core, about belief and identity, about restoring Islam's dignity. In social, legal and political terms, 'it aimed at recapturing the influence Islam had lost in public and social life in the past two centuries, a loss which the Muslim world perceived to result from Westernisation'.[33]

Despite Islamism's formal rejection of the nation-state, it is often nationalism wrapped in the mantle of religion ('Islamo-nationalism', to use the term favoured by some scholars). It is part of a complex and ambivalent response to modernity—an attempt to disentangle modernisation from Westernisation or, to put it another way, to give modernity the legitimacy which in Muslim societies only religion can confer.

An Islamist of the new generation, political scientist Heba Raouf Ezzat, puts it like this: 'We don't have to take the experience of the West and repeat it. We have to make our own present and our own future. I don't have to live in the past of the West, to become in the future what it is now.' She laughs and says she hopes I understand what she means. 'I am against radical Westernisation, in the sense that we should repeat step by step the same course that the West went through—secularisation, urbanisation, industrialisation, all these aspects. I think we have to choose; and I think we have to have the possibility of choosing to reject all that. Why not? Why would it be a taboo?'[34]

More than six decades after the death of Al-Banna, the movement he founded has diversified and has many voices. But for those who are inspired by Al-Banna and Qutb, there remains a fundamental disenchantment with the modern condition of Muslims. The new rulers promised much and all too often turned out to be corrupt, incompetent and repressive. In this respect, the impact of the torture which countless Muslim Brothers endured in Egypt's jails—including Qutb in the 1960s and Zawahiri in the early 1980s—is not to be underestimated. As Hasan Hanafi observed, the Islamists were slow to shake off their 'prison psyche'. It was not just that the scars did not heal. The experience deeply coloured their attitude to the modern state. Using the vocabulary Qutb had given them, they rejected as an abomination the kind of state-worship they believed Nasser and his apparatchiks had fed the masses. Their worldview was Manichean, contrasting the light and truth and justice of Islam with the *jahili* barbarism of the brutal and benighted Arab régimes. They lived, wrote Hanafi, 'in permanent internal and external war'.[35]

Egypt has played a central role in giving birth to the Muslim revolt and keeping it alive. The themes of the Egyptian experience still resonate: fear of the secularising and deracinating effects of Westernisation; a conviction that the traditionalist *ulama* lack solutions to modern problems; an attitude towards the nation-state ranging from reluctant accommodation to outright rejection; and ambivalence about the uses of violence. Each of these themes recurs as the story unfolds.

2

MARTYRS FOR HUSSEIN

Drums beat louder as the procession draws near and in the midday heat the crowd grows expectant. At the head of the procession is a strongman carrying a heavy metal frame known as an *alam*. Some *alams* are fifteen feet wide and weigh as much as 400 kilos. They are decorated with white and coloured plumes and with intricately-made metal animals: a lion, an elephant, a camel and a wingèd horse with the face of a woman—a very Persian creature. Marching behind the *alam* are men and boys dressed in black, chanting and symbolically flaying themselves with a bundle of small chains fixed to a wooden handle.

It is Ashura, the tenth day of the Muslim month of Muharram, and in the suburbs of eastern Tehran everyone has come out to watch. Ashura marks the death and martyrdom of one of the central figures in Shi'ite Islam, Hussein, grandson of the Prophet Muhammad. Hussein was killed in 680 by the forces of the Sunni caliph Yezid in the battle of Karbala, in what is now southern Iraq. The procession symbolises Hussein's army, the *alam* his standard.

Several processions are under way and they converge on a local mosque. The streets are packed. Whatever its religious significance, Ashura is also an extraordinary spectacle, and fun for the family. There are gasps of admiration when the strongman does a little bow in front of the mosque, no easy feat given the width and weight of the *alam*. Then, more daring still, he sends the *alam* slowly spinning round, forcing some of the men in the procession to duck and the crowd to draw back.

An open truck draws up from which a man sprays a fine jet of rosewater from a hose to cool the crowd. My Iranian host and I clamber onto the back of the truck to get a better view. This unfortunately makes me more visible, with my tape recorder and microphone. I'm spotted by a plain-clothes policeman who takes my press card, goes off to phone the Ministry of Culture and Islamic Guidance and does not return for an hour, to my host's irritation and embarrassment. It is a minor brush with an enforcer of the Islamic Republic. But the Ashura celebrations are not imposed by the state. On the contrary, I'm struck by their spontaneous, grass-roots character. The re-enactment of the death of Imam Hussein, Lord of Martyrs, marked every year in processions and passion plays, is the focal point of the culture and identity of the Muslim world's Shi'ite minority.[1]

* * *

The Shi'a are little known and little understood. They account for around fifteen per cent of the world's Muslims. In the Middle East they form majorities only in Iran, Iraq and the island-state of Bahrain. In Lebanon they are the largest minority in a nation of minorities. In Saudi Arabia and the smaller Gulf Arab states, they form minorities often viewed with suspicion by Sunni rulers and the Sunni religious establishment. Further east, there is a Shi'ite majority in Azerbaijan and minorities in India, Pakistan and Afghanistan. Insofar as the Western world is aware of the Shi'a, it is in the form of anti–Western militancy: Iranian crowds chanting 'Death to America', breast-beating Hizbullah fighters in Lebanon and, since 2003, anti–American Shi'ite militias in Iraq, such as the Mahdi Army of the radical young cleric Muqtada al-Sadr.[2]

My first encounter with Shi'ism was in Iraq in the mid-1980s when, as a young journalist, I visited the holy places of Najaf and Karbala. The country was at war with Khomeini's Iran, and its ruler, Saddam Hussein, regarded the Iraqi Shi'a as a fifth column. He gave orders that one of the most prominent Shi'ite scholars, Muhammad Baqer al-Sadr, should be killed and thousands of Shi'a deported to Iran. Perhaps for this reason, he wanted foreign visitors to see for themselves that the situation in the Shi'ite heartland of southern Iraq was firmly under control.

We headed south from Baghdad, our coaches flanked by police outriders. The new motorway passed through flat and featureless terrain, broken here and there by clusters of date-palm and eucalyptus and the occasional débris of a car crash. We crossed the Euphrates, wide and lazy in the midday sun, and there in the distance a golden dome shimmered in the heat haze. Najaf, when you reach it, comes as a shock. It is austere, unwelcoming. 'Unlike Karbala, a place of gardens,' writes Gavin Young in *Iraq: Land of Two Rivers*, 'Najaf has the sterner face of a desert city.'[3]

After the brash modernity of the highway, our coaches and police escort seemed alien and intrusive in the city's narrow and crowded streets. We arrived with brusque suddenness at the entrance to the mosque of Ali, cousin and son-in-law of the Prophet and father of Hussein, the martyr of Karbala. The place was overflowing with people. Women in black stood clutching small children. They were poor, and some of them had come a long way simply to be near Ali's tomb. Ali and Hussein are the central figures in the historical drama of Shi'ism. 'There is no god but God; Muhammad is his Prophet and Ali is the friend of God,' runs the Shi'ite declaration of faith.

There were plenty of soldiers about. The crowds thickened and stared at us with blank faces. Inside the courtyard of the mosque the throng was scarcely any thinner. Small clusters of people squatted on the ground, talking, reading, the women suckling children or simply waiting, patiently, for the saint's benediction. Prominently displayed in the courtyard was a picture of Saddam in pilgrim's garb: an attempt to assert the authority of the state in this most holy of Shi'ite holy places. But as I caught a glimpse, from the outside, of the shrine itself—thick, ornate carpets, glittering chandeliers—I was struck by the sheer magnetic force of this place of pilgrimage and could not help feeling that the state, for all its power, was in awe of it.

Karbala, a few miles north, has a very different setting. On its outskirts we passed prosperous-looking villas, and there was clearly more money about than in tiny Najaf. Karbala's two famous shrines are the tombs of Hussein and Abbas, one of his fiercest generals (known as the Hot-Head) who died alongside him. Outside the tomb of Hussein, a canny photographer was charging pilgrims the equivalent of six dollars to have their picture taken. Inside there was less of a throng than in Najaf and the people looked better off. An old sheikh with a potato nose welcomed us and said the 'brother leader' (Saddam) had recently paid a visit. He had asked the elders how much was needed to keep the shrine in good repair. Six million dollars, they replied. Even if it was ten million, he assured them, they should have it. As a result, the gold of the dome of the mosque had been renewed and the courtyard covered with Italian marble.

As we watched, a coffin was carried in, draped with a red-and-white cloth. It was carried seven times round the tomb before being brought for burial. From the top of the golden dome—flanked by two golden minarets—fluttered a red silk flag, emblem of martyrdom.

* * *

Although Iraq was the site of Shi'ism's holy places, the country the world most closely associated with militant Shi'ism was the Islamic Republic of Iran. A decade later, in 1995, by now working for the BBC, I found myself in Tehran trying to make sense of the Islamic revolution which had so rattled Saddam Hussein. The revolution of 1979 had electrified the whole of the Muslim world and opened up a new phase in the Muslim revolt. Its author, Ayatollah Khomeini, achieved what Hasan al-Banna and Sayyid Qutb had only dreamt of—the creation of an Islamic state.

The Iranian revolution managed to be both Shi'ite and pan-Islamic at the same time. It relied on the unique power and resources of two very Shi'ite (and very Iranian) institutions. The alliance between mosque and bazaar—the 'two lungs of public life'[4]—proved to be the key to Khomeini's success. The merchants and the religious scholars both hated the Shah, providing the only networks of opposition which the régime's notorious secret police, Savak, had been unable to shut down.

The revolution was also Shi'ite in character in that Khomeini was able to exploit the long history of Shi'ite marginalisation and repression in a predominantly Sunni Muslim world. The folk memory of the Shi'a fuses past and present. Their historic grievance dates back to the early years of Islam, when Ali's claim to succeed the Prophet as leader of the Muslims was passed over, precipitating the split between Sunni and Shi'a. Then, over time, as they suffered discrimination at the hands of Sunni rulers, and many Sunni clerics even denounced them as unbelievers, the early sense of grievance was kept alive. In mobilising Iranians against a despotic, irreligious monarch, Khomeini urged them to imitate the spirit of Imam Hussein. The overwhelming feeling of liberation among the Iranian Shi'a in 1979 was as great as that of their Iraqi co-religionists when Saddam Hussein was toppled almost a quarter of a century later.

Yet, for all its Iranian and Shi'ite characteristics, the impact and meaning of Khomeini's revolution were global. Before 1979, despite the Islamic revival and the spread of Islamism in the Middle East and beyond, few had seriously believed it was possible, in the name of Islam, to overthrow an existing government and install a revolutionary new order. For decades, Western social scientists had argued that religion was in decline. Modernisation theory had determined that 'they' (the developing world) would become like 'us' (the developed world) and that, as in the West, religion would gradually decay and become a private matter of little or no significance in public life.

Instead, an elderly, bearded, austere cleric had overthrown a powerful, Western-backed, Western-armed state and forced its autocratic ruler, Muhammad Reza Shah, into humiliating flight. The Shah had, in truth, been his own worst enemy. His grandiose plans for rapid modernisation utilising the country's vast oil and gas wealth—known as the White Revolution—had produced massive dislocation and inequality. Modelling himself, as his father had done, on Turkey's ruthless and successful moderniser, Mustafa Kemal Atatürk, he lacked the all-important legitimacy which Atatürk had gained as victor in Turkey's national liberation struggle. As a result, his efforts to marginalise religion—which, like Atatürk, he regarded as primitive and reactionary—backfired.

The fall of the Shah had huge global ramifications. This reflected the geopolitical reality that Iran is a large and significant country straddling the western and eastern flanks of the Muslim world. The revolution disconcerted both superpowers—the Soviet Union as a neighbouring state nervous of instability on a sensitive border and concerned about its own sizeable Muslim minority; the United States because it had lost a key ally in a major oil-producing country that had played the role of *gendarme* of American policy in the Gulf. The revolution also unnerved Iran's oil-rich Arab neighbours, especially Saudi Arabia, who were close allies of the West, had their own Shi'ite minorities and feared being burnt by the fire of Khomeinism.

For his part, Khomeini was explicit in claiming that his revolution was for all Muslims. His ambition vaulted over the Sunni–Shi'a divide.

* * *

It was not Iran's first revolution. Iranians see the beginning of their modern political history—their Magna Carta moment—in the Constitutional Revolution of 1905–06. By the beginning of the twentieth century Iran had become a pawn in the Great Game, the long-drawn-out struggle for power and influence in Asia waged by the British and Russian empires. 'The Persian court, like a deer feeding two tigers, attempted to preserve its independence by doling out concessions to Britain and Russia even-handedly.'[5] In 1901 the British got the all-important concession to look for oil (though it was not until after the First World War that the first modest revenues started coming in). The influence of these two big powers on Iranian affairs— sometimes in rivalry, sometimes in concert—had a marked influence on the country's political psyche. This was the backdrop to the Constitutional Revolution, which was rooted in deep resentment of foreign penetration of both the court and the economy.

The spark that ignited unrest was the refusal of sugar merchants in the Tehran bazaar to reduce their prices, as the ruler of the day, Shah Muzaffar ad-Din, demanded. When the governor of Tehran ordered that two merchants should suffer the *bastinado*—the indignity of being beaten on the soles of their feet—the bazaar shut down and pent-up demand for an end to autocratic rule welled up in public protest. Mullahs and merchants were weary of a Shah who was 'free to raise cash by selling foreigners economic concessions for everything from tobacco to phonograph records, and a country whose central government was too weak to protect their products from foreign goods or their religion from alien encroachment'.[6]

The Constitutional Revolution was not a purely internal affair. It pitted monarchists backed by Tsarist Russia against liberals supported by the British, whose legation in Tehran they used as a sanctuary, meeting place and open-air university. The revolutionaries—a coalition of mullahs, merchants and intellectuals—pressed the Shah to introduce far-reaching political reforms, including a written constitution and an elected assembly. In 1906 Muzaffar ad-Din finally caved in and approved a newly-drafted constitution. It was the first successful constitutional revolution in the Middle East, serving as a beacon which cast light and shadow on subsequent events.

In name at least, Iran was now a constitutional monarchy with an elected Majlis, or parliament. But neither the Shah and his successors, nor the big powers that exploited them, were ready to accept the new constitutional order. 'Within twelve months Russia and Britain had whittled these hard-won rights to nothing. The monarch returned to being as absolute as he was inefficient and the Majlis degenerated into a marketplace for bribery.'[7]

In 1921 an army officer called Reza Khan seized power, later changing his name to Reza Shah and the country's from Persia to Iran. A giant of a man with little education—Khomeini called him an illiterate soldier—Reza Shah was a tough moderniser in the Atatürk mould. He viewed religion with disdain and saw it as his mission to drag Iran willy-nilly into Western-style modernity. This was made possible by his growing oil revenues, which increased from just over half a million British pounds in 1920 to four million in 1940.[8] This in turn locked Iran more tightly into the embrace of the British empire, whose navy had by now switched from coal to oil. Iran became essential to Britain not only as a buffer against Russian expansion but as a vital source of energy.

During the Second World War, Iranians looked on helplessly as Britain and Russia occupied their country and divided it into zones of influence. In 1941 the occupiers removed Reza Shah, deemed insufficiently anti–German, in favour of his twenty-one-year-old son Muhammad Reza, who was to rule the country until the Khomeini revolution almost four decades later.

The 1950s, when much of the Middle East was in revolt against Western influence, were a crucial decade for Iran. An iconic figure, Muhammad Mossadeq (1882–1967), emerged as the Shah's staunchest nationalist critic. In 1950 Mossadeq, already in his late sixties, was elected prime minister. The following year he nationalised the oil industry. The oil refinery at Abadan, on Iran's southern coast, was Britain's biggest overseas investment. Unwilling to give up so valuable a prize, policy-makers in London plotted 'régime change'. In 1953 the British secret service, MI6, organised a coup in co-operation with the CIA which overthrew Mossadeq and restored the Shah—who had fled the country—to his Peacock Throne. If the events of 1905–06 were a pivotal moment in Iran's struggle against autocratic rule and foreign domination, so too was the drama of the early 1950s, which for Iranians marked a moment of national pride and self-assertion.

Roy Mottahedeh, with characteristic subtlety, sees Mossadeq's challenge to dictatorship in the light of Iranian history: '[He] fulfilled an essential need in the moral drama that Iranians expect to see performed on the political stage. This drama allows Iranians to obey, and sometimes even to admire, the ruling autocrat, but requires that somewhere there be a man of standing who selflessly and tenaciously says "no" to the auto-crat. Many Iranians believe that as long as they quietly, almost surreptitiously, admire the anti–hero, they need not feel that their inner soul has been bought by power.'[9]

This moral drama is a thread running through Iranian and Shi'ite history from the martyrdom of Hussein through the rise and fall of Mossadeq to the Islamic revolution of Ayatollah Khomeini. It expresses the inseparability of the moral and the political, and a deeply ambiguous attitude to power. It is poli-tics as passion play.

* * *

Ruhollah Khomeini was born in a village in central Iran in 1902, the youngest of six children in a family of *sayyids* (cler-ics who claim descent from the Prophet). He studied not only Islamic law but *irfan* (mystical knowledge), which was frowned on by the more orthodox clergy. Indeed, as his views developed, Khomeini was far from conventional. An acknowledged scholar, he was at the same time unorthodox and uncompromising— and in the turbulent years of the Second World War, during the British and Russian occupation, increasingly political.[10]

His real notoriety did not begin, however, until he was sixty and had become a well-known scholar and preacher in the clerical city of Qum. In October 1962 a newspaper reported that the Shah had decided that women should get the vote. It also said that when elected councillors took the oath of office, they would be allowed to swear on 'the holy book', implying that this need not be the Qur'an. Khomeini sent an angry tel-egram to the government declaring that such innovations threatened the Qur'an and Islam. In the face of clerical opposi-tion, the government backed off. But the following year, the Shah returned to the charge, issuing a programme of reform which again included giving the vote to women. Amid protests and clashes, Khomeini was arrested and brought to Tehran.

In 1964 tension increased when parliament was asked to approve a bill giving diplomatic immunity to US military advisers and their staff. When the bill was passed by a slim majority, Khomeini preached a furious sermon denouncing it. 'By this shameful vote, if an American adviser or the servant of an American adviser should take any liberty with one of the greatest specialists in Shi'a law ... the police would have no right to arrest the perpetrator and the courts of Iran have no right to investigate. If the Shah should run over an American dog, he would be called to account but if an American cook should run over the Shah, no one has any claims against him.'[11]

Again Khomeini was arrested, and this time the Shah banished him. He went first to Turkey and then to Iraq, settling in the Shi'ite holy city of Najaf. It was from Najaf that Khomeini issued an influential book on Islamic government and set out the principle of *velayet-e-faqih* (literally, guardianship of the leading jurist), which he was later to use to justify his own pre-eminent role in the affairs of the Islamic Republic.

By 1978 resentment of the Shah had reached boiling point and Khomeini had become his principal opponent-in-exile. Moving from Najaf to Paris, the seventy-six–year-old cleric cunningly gave interviews to the international press hiding his true intentions behind talk of a 'progressive Islam'. In January 1979 the Shah, by now suffering from cancer, left the country. Two weeks later, after fourteen years in exile, Khomeini returned in triumph.

* * *

Tehran nestles at the foot of the Alborz mountains. My fifth-floor room in a hotel otherwise devoid of charm looks out onto snow-capped peaks. Clear mountain water runs in a small channel in the street beneath my balcony. A decade and a half have passed since the revolution, and six years since the death of its founding father.

I attend Friday prayers at Tehran University and find myself sharing the press stand—which affords a bird's eye view of the packed crowd—with television crews from Turkey, Italy and Tajikistan. Many of the men at prayer are wearing black shirts and black trousers for the holy month of Muharram: in a week's time it will be the climactic day of Ashura. As they listen to a succession of speakers, they chant and beat their breasts. Some sob with emotion. Just below me are five men in wheelchairs, veterans of the Iran-Iraq war of the 1980s. Before long there are the ritual chants of 'Death to America', 'Death to Israel'.[12]

On the surface, Khomeinism is alive and well. The ayatollah himself is everywhere present; his name and his speeches are constantly invoked; and it is impossible to escape that stern visage—'a torch shedding black light'[13]—staring down from larger-than-life murals. Yet the heady days of 1979 now seem distant; the early zeal has dissipated.

In 1979 and the early 1980s many Muslims around the world had seen the revolution as nothing less than a turning-point in world history. A young, well-educated Pakistani working for a prestigious European organisation in Islamabad told me the moment Khomeini returned home to take charge of the revolution was the most important day in his life. A young British Muslim who had been a student in 1979 told me how startled his friends had been when he put up a poster of Khomeini in his room, alongside one of his other hero, the rock star Paul Weller. In the Middle East the 1980s were in some respects the Khomeini decade. He dominated the region, a symbol of defiance of the US and Israel and the embodiment of a revolutionary Islam which he contrasted, derisively, with the 'American Islam' of pro-Western Arab régimes. He believed passionately that he would export his revolution, and his enemies believed it too.

In the early days, even as the revolutionaries set about reordering Iranian society, the focus of their energy was on external enemies—the dark alliance of assorted conspirators who were out to crush the revolution in its infancy. Perhaps Khomeini, from his knowledge of Iranian history, knew instinctively that fighting foreign foes would keep the fire of zeal burning. The external enemy meant, first and foremost, America. Anti–Americanism was kept at boiling point not only in the ayatollah's defiant speeches but in the long-drawn-out drama which unfolded when Iranian students seized fifty-two American diplomats and held them hostage in their Tehran embassy from November 1979 to January 1981. The hostage drama, which sank Jimmy Carter's presidency, was America's first direct—and intensely painful—encounter with militant Islam, and it encapsulated the new and deeply antagonistic relationship between Iran and the West. For Khomeini, it served to sharpen the revolutionary fervour of the régime's core constituency: the young, the poor and the *mustazafin*, the dispossessed.

But, before long, a new external enemy loomed. In 1980 the Iraqi leader Saddam Hussein, fearful that the Islamic revolution would infect the Iraqi Shi'a, invaded Iran, plunging the two countries into a debilitating eight-year war. In a sense, this was an extension of the war with America and 'American Islam'. For behind Saddam stood the West and its regional allies, in particular the oil-rich neighbouring states led by Saudi Arabia, who harboured a deep fear of the destabilising impact of Khomeini's revolution. None of these states had much liking for Saddam Hussein, but they saw Iran as the greater threat.

The Iran-Iraq conflict, reminiscent of the First World War in its horror and carnage, not only took a ghastly toll in lives and destruction. It changed the course of the Iranian revolution. The attitude of Iranians, as they watched Khomeini prolong the war Saddam had started, and as they became increasingly aware of the lethal incompetence of their leaders, could never be the same again. It was the end of innocence.[14]

After eight terrible years, Khomeini was forced to drink what he called the 'cup of poison' and accept a ceasefire. His most senior advisers told him he had to choose between the war and the revolution. But in a sense he lost both. By the time of his death the following year, the revolution was in crisis.

* * *

Sitting in the foothills of the Alborz taking black tea and soft dates beside a rushing mountain stream, I heard the uncompromising views of an Iranian academic who had been no friend of the Shah but was blunt in his verdict on those who had succeeded him. Politically, the mullahs had won: they controlled the levers of power and showed no sign of giving them up. What's more, there was no opposition of any consequence. But they had failed to manage the economy—which, given the country's strategic position, large population and massive oil and gas reserves, ought to have been flourishing—or win the hearts and minds of the people. In social terms, they had lost: they had failed to fulfil their revolutionary ambition of creating a new 'Islamic man' and 'Islamic woman'. According to a joke doing the rounds, one Iranian said to another, 'We have been very successful in exporting our revolution.' 'What do you mean?' said the other. 'Because if you look into our houses,' answered the first, 'you won't find a trace of it.'

What had gone wrong? One factor was that Khomeini proved impossible to replace. His role as Supreme Leader was taken by Ayatollah Ali Khamenei, who lacked his charisma and his political and religious authority. The new president, Ali

Akbar Hashemi Rafsanjani, who held the office from 1989 to 1997, sought to carve out a reputation as a pragmatist and a friend of democracy. But he was immensely wealthy and before long his tenure acquired the whiff of corruption. As for his pretensions as a democrat, these were belied by the extra-judicial killings of some eighty dissidents and others during his presidency—something later exposed by one of the most brilliant and outspoken reformist journalists, Akbar Ganji.[15]

The disenchantment engendered by the war with Iraq grew steadily deeper, exacerbated by resentment of corruption, mismanagement of the economy and systematic human-rights abuses. One of the most revealing signs of the times was the disaffection among sections of the clergy. Iran's clerics had always been divided between quietists—who remained aloof from politics, even if that meant *de facto* acquiescence in dictatorial rule—and those like Khomeini who insisted that political activism was intrinsic to Islam. Now even former supporters of the revolution were unhappy over the way it had turned out.

One afternoon a friend drove me in his Paykan—a locally-made version of the Hillman Hunter ubiquitous in Iran long after its disappearance from the streets of Britain—to meet a dissident religious intellectual. Mehdi Ha'eri–Yazdi was a man of two worlds. The son of a famous ayatollah, he had received a religious education in Qum, studying with some of the foremost clerical figures, including Khomeini. Then in the 1960s he had studied and taught at Georgetown, Harvard and Yale, before returning to Iran in 1980 to teach philosophy at Tehran University.

Now in his mid-seventies, he was ill, his voice a whisper. But gradually I grasped the enormity of what he was saying. To the embarrassment of the ruling mullahs, Ha'eri–Yazdi had produced a scathing critique of one of Khomeini's most cherished concepts, the *velayat-e-faqih*, or guardianship of the leading jurist: '*Velayat-e-faqih* as a theory of government [he wrote] has no precedent, and is totally without foundation in *fiqh*, the Islamic law ... these people have formulated the concept of *velayat-e-faqih* in the sense of political sovereignty of the *faqih* (the Islamic jurist), and then by combining it with a republican form of government—which implies the government of the people—have concocted the novel notion of the Islamic Republic under the absolute sovereignty of *velayat-e-faqih*. The outcome ... is an unresolvable paradox which defies reason, logic and human understanding.'[16]

Ha'eri–Yazdi scoffed at the notion that the people needed a guardian. Guardianship was for children and the retarded, he told me with biting irony, not for adult human beings. If the editor of a liberal newspaper had published such heretical views, he would have been arrested and his paper shut down. But Ha'eri–Yazdi was the son of a respected Islamic scholar and had a degree of immunity. His critique was all the sharper for coming from within. Moreover he was not alone. Other clerics, including some senior figures, were speaking out against the excesses of the régime.

* * *

Between 1968 and 1988 Iran's population had doubled from twenty-seven million to fifty-five million. Two-thirds of its people were under thirty-three. An increasingly urbanised population felt its most basic needs were not being met. Faced with the social consequences of this population explosion—exacerbated by the pressures of the war with Iraq—Khomeini had performed a U-turn and issued a *fatwa* authorising birth control. As a result, the growth rate was reduced to one of the lowest in the Middle East. Even so, the Islamic Republic was left struggling to meet the demands of a large and youthful population.[17] Coping with a pool of restless young men and women was not a problem unique to Iran, but for a régime which claimed a religious mandate it posed particular problems. State-sanctioned vigilantes periodically tried to enforce the (widely-flouted) ban on satellite dishes and the dress code for women—the all-enveloping chador which is not only dowdy but in the summer months unbearably hot. They also broke up parties to prevent young people listening to Western music, drinking alcohol and taking drugs—easily and cheaply available from neighbouring Afghanistan.

The Islamic Republic had not eliminated sex, drugs and rock and roll, merely driven them underground. It had also alienated women and the young by turning the clock back with regard to women's rights. I went to see the lawyer Shirin Ebadi, a fearless human-rights campaigner who was subsequently awarded the Nobel Peace Prize. In the Shah's day she had been a judge. But after the revolution women were not allowed to be judges. She described the Kafkaesque world of the ayatollahs' justice system.

'A girl is considered mature enough to get married at the age of nine. But she's not considered mature enough to vote until she's fifteen. The age of criminal responsibility is nine. If a girl of nine commits a crime she will be tried as a mature and competent person, just like a man of forty—and she could be sentenced to death. But if the same girl wants to apply for a passport, she has to secure the permission of her father.

'A woman can start working at the age of fifteen. If she's under fifteen, she can't work; that would be considered exploitation. But she can marry. And if she's to work, she has to work at home. Even if her husband is disabled, she can't work outside the home.

'What kind of justice is that?'[18]

***

Then, two years later, in 1997, something unexpected happened. The war of attrition—sometimes overt, sometimes hidden from view—between the reformist and conservative wings of the religious establishment came to a head in what many saw as a revolution within the revolution: the surprise election of a reformist president, Muhammad Khatami.

On election day I travelled to the polling stations in my translator's old Peugeot and watched as enthusiastic first-time voters flocked to vote, sometimes dragging mum and dad along as well. One woman told me the election was a contest between the open mind and the closed mind. Khatami belonged to the clerical élite, but he was also a highly-educated liberal; he even smiled. Most people I spoke to believed fatalistically that the authorities would make sure his rival, the conservative speaker of parliament, was victorious. Instead, Khatami won by a landslide.

It was a remarkable moment of people power. 'In some ways,' writes the Iranian historian Ervand Abrahamian, 'the clock had been turned back to the Constitutional Revolution.'[19] The people had voted for a more open and democratic Iran, with more room to breathe. They wanted the mullahs to relax their irksome restrictions on daily life. They wanted a government that would curb inflation and unemployment and deal with endemic corruption. And they wanted—or some of them wanted—an opening-up to the outside world, perhaps even the normalisation of relations with America.

After the election, I attended the new president's first press conference. Christiane Amanpour of CNN got to ask the first question, the BBC the second. What is the difference, I asked, between the 'Islamic civil society' you are advocating and civil society as it is generally understood? Khatami's answer was polite but evasive: we want a civil society in an Islamic context.

Khatami was popular and well-intentioned; he ignited hope for change among ordinary Iranians and in the outside world.

For a while, reformists dominated the parliament and some of the ministries and became a lively presence within the media and in cultural life. Abroad, Khatami promoted the idea of a 'dialogue of civilisations' as a riposte to Samuel Huntington's 'clash of civilisations'. In 2001 he was elected for a second term: a sign that the thirst for change had not been slaked.

But well before the end of his eight-year presidency (1997–2005), it was clear the reformist project had failed. Eventually, the acid prediction of an Iranian friend on the night of Khatami's first election victory proved correct: 'The system will devour him.' I had been unwilling to believe it at the time, but the cynicism proved to be justified. It took time, but little by little the reformists' conservative rivals regained the upper hand. Many liberals believed that President Bush undermined their position when he made a speech in 2002 linking Iran, Iraq, North Korea and 'their terrorist allies' in an 'axis of evil'. This destroyed whatever chance there might have been that, after 9/11, the US and Iran would find common cause in opposing the Sunni extremism of the Taliban and Al-Qaeda.

The conservatives, no less powerful for being (for the most part) unelected, clawed back the influence they had lost in 1997. They blocked reformist legislation, locked up liberal newspaper editors, shut down their publications and sent hooligans to break up meetings addressed by free-thinking intellectuals.

One of these intellectuals was Abdelkarim Soroush, among Iran's most influential Muslim thinkers. I went to hear him speak at a packed meeting of students at one of Tehran's universities. Soroush was not a cleric, but in the early days of the revolution he had played a leading role in the 'cultural revolution' (the purging of staff, the re-writing of curricula) in the universities. Over time, however, he had become increasingly critical of clerical rule. His books, lectures and articles, avidly read in Iran and among a large Muslim following outside the country, addressed fundamental issues of Islam and modernity. Soroush distinguished between the divine nature of the Qur'anic revelation and the fallible nature of human knowledge. This implicitly dethroned the religious scholars, since scholarly knowledge of the religious texts was human, not divine. Soroush believed that, in principle, Islam and democracy were compatible. He believed Muslims should be governed according to Islamic precepts but did not believe this task should be entrusted to the clergy. In this respect, he had shaken one of the central pillars of the Islamic revolution.[20]

To hear what Soroush's critics had to say, I visited the office of a conservative newspaper, *Sobh*, and over tea and cakes talked to its bearded young editor, Mehdi Nassiri. He was highly critical of the Western media—including the BBC—and believed Islam must make no compromise with the new world order. He dismissed Soroush as one of a long line of misguided individuals who had promoted a 'liberal' Islam. Liberalism proclaimed the sovereignty of man, he declared emphatically, whereas Islam proclaimed the sovereignty of God: the two were utterly incompatible. This was vintage Khomeinism; the hard-liners viewed themselves as keepers of the revolutionary flame.

The leading reformist thinkers were impressive. But as the conservative resurgence gathered pace, several of them, including Soroush, were forced to leave the country and those that remained suffered severe restrictions. One of the most outspoken clerical dissidents was Mohsen Kadivar, who had been twenty at the time of the revolution and one of its active supporters. A few months after Khatami's election in 1997, however, he had published an outspoken newspaper article declaring that the people had voted against 'the governmental religion (*din-e dawlati*), privileged-classism (*qeshrgeri*), violence, wisdom-bashing, despotism of opinion, and populist society'.[21] As a result, he had been forced out of his teaching position at Imam Sadeq University in Tehran.

Since then, Kadivar had been repeatedly imprisoned for denouncing the regime's repressive behaviour and challenging head-on the principle of *velayet-e-faqih*, which enshrined the hegemony of the Supreme Leader. Kadivar had used his imprisonment to write books. He was that rare thing, a consistent liberal. He argued, for example, that it was just as wrong for the authorities in Iran to make women wear the *hijab* as for the Turkish authorities to make them take it off. (He would *prefer* Muslim women to wear it, but was against compulsion.) When I suggested that reformists like him were nice guys who were hopelessly outgunned, he replied that they had the majority of the people behind them. But a few years after our meeting, he too was forced into exile, in the United States.[22]

In 2004 the conservatives regained control of parliament, and the following year a little-known figure—a populist conservative, Mahmoud Ahmadi–Nejad, the son of a blacksmith—became president after defeating the more pragmatic Hashemi Rafsanjani. This marked the entrenchment of the conservatives and heightened the sense of confrontation with the West over Iran's growing influence in the Middle East and its ambition to become a nuclear power. In June 2009 Ahmadi–Nejad won a second term in what were widely seen as fraudulent elections. This provoked mass protests and the most serious crisis of legitimacy since the revolution.

***

How are we to assess the Iranian revolution, three decades on? In the land of its birth, it has been singularly unsuccessful. Viewed as a laboratory of Islamic government, it has failed to come up with convincing solutions to the political, economic and social problems of a modern Muslim society. The Islamic

Republic's human-rights abuses rival those of the Shah and his secret police. Far from winning hearts and minds, the ruling mullahs have alienated many of their own original supporters. Some argue that, in seeking to marry religion and politics, they have actually discredited Islam.

Yet outside Iran, although the early excitement of Khomeini's achievement has faded, his revolution and its legacy still count for something. In the story of the Muslim revolt from Hasan al-Banna until today, it is an important milestone. While Islamists have governed elsewhere—the Taliban in Afghanistan, Hasan al-Turabi in Sudan, Hamas in Gaza, in each case without conspicuous success—the Iranian revolution remains the single most important experiment in Islamic government in modern times. The core values of the revolution—social justice, independence, self-sufficiency, piety—still resonate with Muslims who compare their own governments unfavourably with Iran's and cling to the belief that, in the complex societies of the twenty-first century, Islam is the solution to their problems.[23]

Is there, then, an Iranian—or Shi'ite—model of militant Islam? Even in its post-revolutionary phase, Iran still exerts an influence in the Middle East and the wider Muslim world. To some extent, its enemies have helped. In its approach to the Middle East, the Bush administration (2000–08) unwittingly boosted the regional power and prestige of the Islamic Republic. Iran extended its influence in three sensitive arenas: Iraq, Lebanon and the Palestinian territories. The US-led invasion of Iraq in 2003 overturned the regional balance of power in Iran's favour. It disposed of one of the Iranian régime's most hated enemies, Saddam Hussein—still remembered by Iranians as the author of the Iran-Iraq war of the 1980s—and put in his place a government dominated by Iraqi Shi'ite politicians with links to Tehran.

At the same time, Iran's ally Hizbullah—the Shi'ite movement it had helped create in response to Israel's invasion of Lebanon in 1982—succeeded in strengthening its position as one of the main players in the complicated Lebanese political scene. Iran's support for the militant Palestinian group Hamas gave it a new leverage in the Arab-Israeli dispute. Does Iran also have the ability to spark revolt among the Shi'a minorities in Saudi Arabia and the smaller Gulf Arab monarchies? These minorities have grievances of long standing which have been aggravated as sectarian tensions in Iraq have spread beyond its borders. But the Arab Shi'a remain Arab. They have a sense of belonging to the states where they live, and the notion that they are cat's paws of Iran is misleading.

How far Iran's influence—and for that matter Hizbullah's—extends beyond the Middle East is open to debate. The Bush administration was inclined to see both as players with 'global reach'—an important distinction since it put the Iran-Syria-Hizbullah axis on a par with Al-Qaeda and the global Sunni jihadists. Both Iran and Hizbullah were by all accounts involved in attacks in the 1990s against Jewish and Israeli targets in Argentina, and Hizbullah retains networks of support in both North and South America.[24] Within the Middle East their main—but not exclusive—focus has been on the anti–Israeli struggle. Both stand accused of involvement in the attack in 1996 against a US military residential compound in Al-Khobar, in eastern Saudi Arabia.[25] And after the invasion of Iraq in 2003, Iran supported Iraqi Shi'ite militias with arms, money and training, in order to maintain pressure on American and British forces there.

Clearly, some Sunnis—not least jihadists loyal to Al-Qaeda—view Iran and Hizbullah with the deepest suspicion. In the climate of sectarianism which infected Middle East politics following the upsurge in Sunni–Shi'a violence in Iraq in 2005–06, some Sunni clerics saw Iran as a sinister and aggressive force in the region. How far this reached the grass roots, however, is another matter. When Israel fought an unsuccessful month-long war against Hizbullah in the summer of 2006, the Hizbullah leader Hasan Nasrallah became the hero of the Arab street and Iran's role in championing the anti–Israeli struggle was widely applauded. Especially at moments of crisis, hostility to Israel tends to trump sectarian loyalty.

Overall, Iran's influence as a role model for Islamic militancy is largely symbolic. While at home the Islamic Republic is deeply discredited, among Muslims elsewhere, Sunni as well as Shi'a, it still has the power to inspire.

This is the Iranian paradox.[26]

3

CULTURE OF *JIHAD*

A chunk of the Berlin Wall sits in Hamid Gul's living-room, a gift for services rendered during the Cold War. General Gul himself is, to all outward appearances, the embodiment of the Pakistani officer class. Receiving me at his comfortable bunga-low in the military cantonment in Rawalpindi, on the edge of the capital Islamabad, he is impeccably dressed in blazer and tie. He speaks the pukka English of the educated of the Indian sub-continent. But appearances can deceive. Gul is a fervent Islamist, a supporter of the Taliban and admirer of Osama bin Laden, who has played a not inconsequential role in Pakistan's passage from Cold War to holy war.[1]

* * *

Pakistan is the only country created in the name of Islam. It emerged from the chaotic, blood-stained partition of India in 1947 as a homeland for the Muslims of the sub-continent. Whether that made it an Islamic state or merely a state for Muslims has been hotly debated ever since.

From the moment of its birth, the connection between reli-gion and national identity has been problematic. The father of the new state, the British-educated lawyer Muhammad Ali Jin-nah (1876–1948), was a secular liberal who regarded Islam as part of the cultural heritage and hence as a building-block of nationhood. He dreamt of a Muslim renaissance in the sub-

continent but wanted the new Pakistan to be a modern, tolerant country where minorities would enjoy equality under the
law. There is no evidence that he favoured the imposition of
the Shari'a (Islamic law) or viewed Islam in ideological terms.
On the contrary, he declared in a speech on the eve of independence: 'You are free, free to go to your temples; you are
free to go to your mosques or to any other places of worship
in this state of Pakistan. You may belong to any religion or
caste or creed—that has nothing to do with the business of the
state [Hear, Hear] ...

'We are starting in the days,' he went on, 'when there is no
discrimination, no distinction between one community and
another ... We are starting with this fundamental principle
that we are all citizens and equal citizens of one State [Loud
Applause] ... Now I think you should keep that in front of us
as our ideal, and you will find that in course of time Hindus
would cease to be Hindus and Muslims would cease to be
Muslims, not in the religious sense, because that is the personal
faith of each individual, but in the political sense as citizens of
the State.'[2]

Since Jinnah's untimely death in 1948, there has been a tug-
of-war over his legacy. Islamists such as Hamid Gul argue that
when he referred to citizens being equal under the law, he
meant Islamic law. This is unconvincing. But whatever the
personal preferences of Pakistan's founding father—the Quaid-
i–Azam, or Great Leader, as he is known—he succeeded in
placing Islam squarely at the centre of the country's existence,
and after his death it was left to others to define what precisely
that would mean. Since then, Pakistan has experienced three
wars with India, the breakaway of Bangladesh (formerly East
Pakistan), four military interventions and an unresolved crisis
of identity. Rather than becoming a force for national unity,
religion has all too often been a source of division. While most

Pakistanis reject Islamism—something they have consistently shown through the ballot-box—a number of small religious parties have acquired disproportionate influence and formed tactical alliances with leaders who lacked popular support. Successive military rulers, from Ayub Khan to Pervez Musharraf, have needed legitimacy and 'by virtue of their inescapably dubious claim to power, [were] sooner or later driven to ... garb themselves in Islam'.[3]

But while Pakistan's rulers have to varying degrees exploited Islam, only one used it systematically as the ideology of state and society. This was General Muhammad Zia ul-Haq, whose eleven-year rule from 1977 to 1988 was distinguished by his personal commitment to Islamisation and by an accident of geopolitics. A convergence of events in Saudi Arabia, Iran and Afghanistan conspired to propel Pakistan into a front-line role in the fateful Muslim *jihad* of the 1980s.

General Zia was fifty-two when, as army chief of staff, he seized power, declaring martial law and ousting Zulfikar Ali Bhutto (father of the future prime minister Benazir), who was subsequently tried and hanged. It was the third military intervention since the country's creation three decades earlier. Justifying his action, the general declared in a speech to the nation, 'When political leaders fail to steer the country out of a crisis, it is an inexcusable sin for the armed forces to sit as silent spectators.' In a harbinger of things to come, he invoked the 'spirit of Islam' as the key to Pakistan's survival as a nation. An early report on the coup, by Edward Behr of *Newsweek*, quoted one of Zia's admirers as saying, 'He is deeply religious without any element of fanaticism. He genuinely seems to believe that the motivation of inner religious faith would be a strong element in improving the army's morale.' The report noted that he had made known his displeasure with fellow Muslim officers who drank alcohol.[4]

Zia promised there would be elections, and then postponed them. It soon became apparent that he intended to use Islam as the unifying thread of his policies. To some extent the ground had been prepared during the six–year rule of his predecessor, Zulfikar Ali Bhutto, who had for reasons of political expediency promoted what he called 'Islamic socialism'. Bhutto cynically banned alcohol and gambling, made Friday a day of rest, used the rhetoric of Islamic unity in his foreign policy and supported moves to declare the hapless Ahmadi sect un-Islamic.[5] (The Ahmadis consider themselves Muslims, but do not share the orthodox view of Muhammad as the last of the prophets.)

But Zia went much further. In February 1979—the month Ayatollah Khomeini returned home to Iran from exile in France—the general declared, 'I am today formally announcing the introduction of the Islamic system in the country.' In inaugurating his programme of Islamisation, Zia was careful to invoke the name of Jinnah. In fact his 'Islamic system' (*nizam-i–islam*) was more radical than anything Jinnah could ever have envisaged or wanted.

Zia's reforms entailed the instilling of Islamic values (as he perceived them) into the education system, into the army (under the motto 'Faith, Obedience to God and Jihad in the Service of Allah'), into the economy—which he sought to rid of the 'curse of interest'—and into the legal system, where he introduced the controversial *hudud* punishments, including amputation for theft and flogging for adultery. (These punishments shocked liberal Pakistanis and the outside world even though they were seldom carried out.) In addition, he created an infrastructure of well-funded Islamic institutions, including mosques and *madrasas* (seminaries).

The effects were far-reaching. Zia entangled the military in politics to a new degree, creating an 'invisible trinity' of religion, the state and the military.[6] He also significantly tilted the balance between a new, hard-edged form of Sunni Islam and an older and more tolerant tradition, tinged with mysticism, which had for centuries been deeply embedded among the Muslims of the sub-continent.

***

Visit the Badshahi mosque in the old city of Lahore, and you cannot fail to be struck by the historic splendour of Islam in the Indian sub-continent. Built of red sandstone and white marble, it is one of the most spectacular mosques anywhere in the world, able to accommodate 100,000 worshippers. Its construction dates from the seventeenth century—the high point of the Mughal empire.

The Mughal emperors ruled a large part of India, as a Muslim dynasty governing a Hindu majority, from the early sixteenth century until they were displaced by the British Raj some 300 years later. Their names—Babur, Humayun, Akbar, Jahangir, Shah Jahan, Aurangzeb—are associated with wealth and glittering literary and artistic achievement, exemplified in the Taj Mahal, built in 1648 by Shah Jahan, and the Badshahi mosque constructed twenty-five years later by his son Aurangzeb. Proud Muslim parents from India and Pakistan, including those living in the West, still name their sons after these Great Mughals. Akbar, the greatest of them, who reigned for half a century from 1556 to 1605, extended the borders of the empire, made Persian the official language of court, encouraged inter-marriage with Hindus and, to the consternation of the orthodox religious scholars, turned away from traditional Islam to a tolerant and syncretic religion of his own. But by the time Aurangzeb died in 1707, signs of decline were already apparent. The middle of the eighteenth century ushered in a period of British expansion and Mughal eclipse.[7]

'Islam in the Indian sub-continent,' writes the historian Aziz Ahmad, 'has had two external challenges which could threaten its identity, the Hindu and the Western.' It was strong enough to resist 'Hinduism's assimilative pull'; but the British empire was another matter.[8] During two centuries of British rule, the Muslims of India faced essentially the same set of choices that confronted Egyptian Muslims in roughly the same period: whether to accept European-style modernity, reject it in defence of the faith or try to produce some sort of synthesis. But while Egypt was relatively homogeneous, India had somehow to come to terms with its cultural and religious diversity. With the birth of Pakistan, the Muslims of the sub-continent achieved independence (or most of them, with a substantial minority remaining in India) but faced severe political, economic and social handicaps.

Jinnah saw the Mughal period as a kind of golden age and wanted a successful and enlightened Pakistan to regain some of its lustre. But today liberal Pakistanis like Suroosh Irfani contrast what they regard as the tolerant multi–culturalism of the Mughals with the narrow-minded Islamism they associate with General Zia. Irfani teaches at a liberal arts college in Lahore. He is an eloquent advocate of Sufism, the mystical and sometimes heterodox tradition in Islam which flourished both before and during the Mughal era and still retains a hold on the hearts and minds of Muslims in the sub-continent, especially in rural areas.

'Sufism has been central to the Islam of the sub-continent,' Irfani argues. 'Central in the sense that the spread of Islam came about through the work of the Sufis—Sufis as teachers, as travelling preachers, as singers—and Sufi orders, Sufi networking, which provided social services, healthcare for the homeless, free food, lodges for the travellers.' He cites as a witness the thirteenth-century Muslim traveller Ibn Battuta, who wrote that when he travelled across India to China he stayed in a different Sufi lodge every night.[9]

On a sultry Thursday night, a Pakistani friend takes me to the Shah Jamal shrine in Lahore. Shah Jamal was a Sufi saint from the Mughal period. A crowd has gathered expectantly in a courtyard near the shrine. Many have come from the surrounding villages. Boys climb trees to get a better view. Men are selling chapatis laced with hashish. The star of the night, Pappoo, is dressed in a bright red robe with a long cylindrical drum, known as a *dhol*, tied to his neck. At first he stands on one side, biding his time. Then he moves into the centre of the courtyard, shooing the crowd back to make space. Gradually he begins to whirl and chant and beat the drum with a metal hook, each drumbeat like the crack of a gunshot. As he chants, the crowd chants back. He whirls faster and faster, in a trance-like state, sweat pouring down his face, producing a wild climax of heat and dust and sound and spectacle.

This is folk Islam—and the orthodox frown on it. They disapprove not only of music and dancing (and hashish) but of the very notion of revering saints, which for them is *shirk* (idolatry). There has long been a tension in the sub-continent between the Islam of the mosque—and in particular the Deobandi form of Sunni Islam which emerged during the British Raj—and the lively, popular Islam of the shrine, whose followers are known as Barelwis. Numerically, the Barelwi trend is probably still dominant, but Zia dramatically empowered the rival Deobandis. From the late 1970s, relying on generous aid from Saudi Arabia, he poured money into the building and expansion of Deobandi *madrasas* and other institutions.

At the same time he formed an alliance with Sunni Islamist parties which had traditionally enjoyed little electoral backing but were supporters and beneficiaries of his Islamisation policies. The most important of these was the Jamaat-i–Islami, which had been founded at the time of the Second World War by one of the most influential twentieth-century Islamist ideologues, Abul-Ala Maududi (1903–79). Unlike Jinnah, Maududi saw Islam as a political system rather than just part of a cultural heritage.

Born in undivided India, he worked as a journalist and was at first an enthusiastic Indian nationalist. Only later did he turn his back on nationalism to embrace the idea of an Islamic state under the sovereignty of God. As such, he opposed the creation of Pakistan, accusing Jinnah of being ensnared by the 'false idol' of nationalism;[10] indeed he created the Jamaat in 1941 as a rival to Jinnah's Muslim League. Once an independent Pakistan had emerged, however, he was pragmatic enough to establish himself there and campaign to turn his vision of the Islamic state into a reality. He played much the same role in south Asia as Hasan al-Banna did in the Middle East, turning the Jamaat into a kind of Asian version of the Muslim Brotherhood. But he went further than Al-Banna in creating a blueprint for the Islamic state.

I visited one of Maududi's disciples, Anis Ahmad, in 1995 at the International Islamic University in Islamabad. The university adjoins the King Faisal Mosque, a work of jutting modernity with four rocket-like minarets. The mosque was designed by a Turkish architect in the 1970s (during Bhutto's rule), completed in 1986 and paid for by Saudi Arabia. It can accommodate 300,000 worshippers (three times more than the Badshahi mosque in Lahore). The university, with some 14,000 students from all over the world, is considered a Jamaati stronghold.

Dr Ahmad, who with his brother Khurshid is a well-known figure within the movement, is a small, neat, American-educated professor who wears sneakers. He explains why Maududi's thought was innovative: 'He is not for the traditional

Islam. He is not for the so-called revolutionary Islam. But he is for going back to the sources and then applying reason in order to discover contemporary solutions. So his approach is essentially the *ijtihadi* approach. The term *ijtihad* in Islam stands for innovation—but innovation which has a relationship with tradition. So Maududi stands for *ijtihad* in mass communication, or *da'wa*; *ijtihad* in legal matters, or Shari'a; *ijtihad* in political matters; *ijtihad* in ethical matters.'[11]

This paints Maududi as an enlightened progressive trying to blend tradition and modernity. Others, however, see him as a utopian with totalitarian tendencies, at war with what he termed 'un-Islam'. As one authority on the Jamaat puts it, Maududi regarded 'the battle between Islam and un-Islam (*kufr*)—the West as well as the traditional [Sufi] Muslim culture of India—as the central force in the historical progression of Muslim societies ... The struggle between Islam and un-Islam ... would culminate in an Islamic revolution and the creation of an Islamic state, which would in turn initiate large-scale reforms in society, leading to a utopian Islamic order'.[12]

It was Maududi who first used the term *jahiliyya*—signifying the forces of ignorance and barbarism—which Sayyid Qutb in Egypt made famous, with a distinctly more radical twist, in his influential book *Milestones*. The vanquishing of un-Islam would usher in a new order imposed by a specially-trained Muslim élite—an Islamist avant-garde—that would win power by whatever means were necessary. While not explicitly advocating violence, Maududi did not rule it out.

This totalitarian vision of Islam-from-above (in contrast to Al-Banna's vision of Islam-from-below) chimed perfectly with that of General Zia. Indeed Maududi lived long enough to give his blessing to Zia's 'Islamic system'. Zia in turn accorded him the status of elder statesman which he enjoyed until his death in 1979. During Zia's rule the Jamaat enjoyed a new political influence. Its leaders held government posts, including cabinet positions, and played a direct role in the Islamisation of the country. But the party paid a price for being co-opted by Zia, and was later dogged by the charge that it had given a cover of religious legitimacy to a military dictatorship.[13]

* * *

In a colonnade on one side of a brightly-painted courtyard, a group of boys sit cross-legged making a babble of sound as they recite the Qur'an. This is a *madrasa*—a word that has become, unjustly, synonymous with the indoctrination of bigotry and violence. In fact this is a Barelwi *madrasa* in Lahore, with some 1,400 students aged between ten and twenty-four, which I visit in the spring of 2002. Its director, Dr Muhammad Naeemi, rejects the charge that he teaches extremism and resents the efforts of the government of Pervez Musharraf—the general who had seized power in 1999—to bring *madrasas* under tighter control. (After the attacks of 9/11, Musharraf repeatedly pledged to bring the *madrasas* into line, but failed to do so.)

My efforts to visit a notorious Deobandi *madrasa* are unsuccessful: in the current atmosphere of confrontation between the government and the *madrasas* the foreign press are not welcome. But I begin to understand why these institutions flourish: they help fill the gaping void of public education in a country where only three per cent of the national budget is spent on education, health and public welfare, while the military accounts for a quarter. Tales abound of schools without books, desks or equipment, and even of 'ghost schools' where someone draws a salary but there are no students. Besides, many parents in the poorer villages of rural Pakistan are happy to have their sons given free food and lodging while being trained, notionally at least, as future *imams*.[14]

The role of the Deobandi *madrasas* changed dramatically as a result of Zia's project of Islamisation. That project might have remained a largely Pakistani affair had the Soviet Union not invaded neighbouring Afghanistan on Christmas Eve 1979, provoking the last great battle of the Cold War. Zia was quick to see that the Russian gamble—in retrospect a blunder which helped bring about the eventual demise of the Soviet Union—gave Pakistan a unique geopolitical opportunity.

First under Jimmy Carter and then more full-bloodedly under Ronald Reagan, the United States armed and funded the Afghan *mujahidin* (holy warriors) who were resisting Soviet occupation. At the same time Washington's Arab allies, notably Saudi Arabia and Egypt, helped mobilise an international army of Muslim volunteers to fight alongside the Afghans. Pakistan became the conduit and beneficiary of the huge quantities of money and weapons supplied to the *mujahidin* by the United States, Saudi Arabia and others. It was suddenly a major player on the Cold War stage. Turning its *madrasas* into factories of *jihad*—churning out both Pakistani and Afghan holy warriors—fitted in with Zia's strategy of Islamisation at home and Islamisation abroad. There had been fewer than 1,000 *madrasas* in Pakistan before he seized power; by the time of his death in 1988 there were 8,000; by 2009 there were thought to be more than 20,000 (though there is much debate about their numbers and how many students they have). Part of Zia's strategy was to site many of the new *madrasas* in the north-west of the country so that their graduates could cross and re-cross the Afghan border at will.[15]

The role of one leading Deobandi *madrasa* is instructive. The Jamiat al-Ulum al-Islamiyya, founded in Karachi in 1955, has played a central role in some of the country's most contentious issues and crises. Under its founder, Muhammad Yusuf Banuri, it campaigned successfully for the Ahmadi minority to be officially declared non-Muslim. The college—popularly known as the Banuri Town Madrasa—attacked a distinguished advocate of Islamic modernism, the scholar Fazlur Rahman, who was eventually forced into exile. And under Banuri's successors, the Jamiat became involved in anti–Shi'a sectarian politics in Pakistan and in supporting both the Muslim struggle in Kashmir and the anti–Soviet war in Afghanistan. 'Of all the Pakistani *madrasas*,' writes Muhammad Qasim Zaman, a scholar of Islamic education, 'the Jamiat al-Ulum's reputation for militant activism is surely the best deserved.'[16]

Zia entrusted the management of the war to his military intelligence service, the Inter-Services Intelligence (ISI) directorate, which had been created in 1948 and now acquired an altogether new power and prestige. In doing so he gave a largely secular institution a more pronounced Islamic character. It was the ISI which funnelled weapons and money to the seven-party Afghan *mujahidin* alliance, favouring its more militantly Islamist members.[17] Zia moulded a military leadership in his own image, promoting men like Hamid Gul and uniting them behind a strategy with four main components: hostility and suspicion towards India, support for the Muslims of Indian-ruled Kashmir, development of nuclear weapons and the promotion of a friendly (or at least unthreatening) régime in Afghanistan. Despite the exigencies of the post-9/11 era, all of these aims have survived as the military's core strategic objectives.

The Afghan conflict brought together an extraordinarily diverse Cold War alliance. At its heart was the troika of Ronald Reagan, Zia ul-Haq and the Saudi ruler King Fahd.[18] The CIA spent $6 billion in backing the *mujahidin* and the Saudis matched them dollar for dollar. ('We don't do operations,' Prince Turki al-Faisal, the head of Saudi intelligence, told a CIA colleague. 'We don't know how. All we know how to do is write cheques.')[19] Soviet costs in maintaining an occupation force of 100,000 troops and in propping up the Afghan government and its armed forces were even higher. Other actors assisted the troika in a variety of ways: the Europeans, including Margaret Thatcher's Britain and François Mitterrand's France, the Chinese, the Egyptians—even, covertly, the Israelis.

The war was a turning-point which radicalised and internationalised the Muslim revolt, drawing young Muslims from many countries to a battle whose consequences few foresaw. The story of one young man from North Africa is typical of many. One day in 1984 a twenty-five-year-old Algerian, Abdullah Anas, read in a magazine about a *fatwa* (religious ruling) declaring it was every Muslim's duty to help the people of Afghanistan fight the Soviet invaders. He heeded the call, even though, as he told me later, he knew almost nothing about Afghanistan and would have had difficulty finding it on a map.

Like many of the Arab volunteers, Anas came under the spell of Abdullah Azzam (1941–89), a charismatic Palestinian sometimes known as the 'godfather of *jihad*'. Azzam ran the Office of Services, a reception centre for would-be holy warriors in Peshawar, the Pakistani town which served as the launching-pad for *mujahidin* operations inside Afghanistan. The bond became closer when the young Algerian married one of Azzam's daughters. Azzam's most famous protégé was a wealthy young Saudi, Osama bin Laden, who visited Peshawar regularly as a sponsor and cheerleader of the anti–Soviet *jihad*. Anas recalls him as someone with charisma rather than political sophistication. 'He ate very little. He slept very little. Very generous. He'd give you his clothes. He'd give you his money.' As for his powers of persuasion: 'When you sit with Osama, you don't want to leave the meeting. You wish to continue talking to him because he is very calm, very fluent.'[20]

But Anas and Bin Laden found themselves on opposing sides when the Arab contingent split apart during the final years of the war. On one side stood Azzam and his supporters who believed *jihad* was only legitimate when Muslims were under foreign occupation (in Afghanistan or Palestine or Kashmir). On the other were Bin Laden and his followers who were already contemplating something far more radical: a global *jihad* against the United States and the 'infidel' régimes of the Muslim world.

Azzam and Anas were convinced Bin Laden was being led astray by his Egyptian allies, above all by Ayman al-Zawahiri. The dispute was bitter. After Zawahiri spread rumours that Azzam was working for the Americans, Azzam and two of his sons were killed in a car-bomb attack in 1989, in circumstances that have never been explained. Anas tried to take over Azzam's organisation but the more militant faction seized control and established what was to become Al-Qaeda. 'They loved the ideas of Osama and the person of Abdullah Azzam,' Anas recalled wistfully. 'They don't love me.'[21]

* * *

Hamid Gul was in the thick of it. In 1987 Zia promoted him to head the ISI, a position from which he directed aid to the most radical *mujahidin* groups fighting the Soviet forces. Gul worked closely with both the Americans and Saudi Arabia's Prince Turki al-Faisal. According to Steve Coll in *Ghost Wars*, a prize-winning account of the Afghan war and the rise of Al-Qaeda, the Americans at first saw Gul as pro-Western. A report by the US Defence Intelligence Agency described him as a Westernised, alcohol-imbibing friend of the United States and a reliable partner in the fight against communism. But at some point—for reasons that are not entirely clear—this 'smooth chameleon', as Coll calls him, became a radical Islamist and passionately anti–American.[22]

In 1988 the *mujahidin* and their Islamist backers in the ISI lost one of their most powerful patrons when Zia, together with a number of top Pakistani and US officials, died in a mysterious plane crash. Democracy was restored under a thirty-five-year-old Benazir Bhutto, who mistrusted the ISI and believed, with some reason, that it was out to undermine her. In 1989 she fired Gul from his position as head of the ISI. He eventually retired from the army but remained influential, building links with both the Taliban and Bin Laden. Coll believes the public humiliation of being dismissed by a woman prime minister whom he disliked and resented may have contributed to his radicalisation.

By now the futility of the Russian occupation of Afghanistan was clear. The Soviet leader Mikhail Gorbachev decided it was time for his forces to get out. In 1989, after a decade in the Afghan 'bear trap', they withdrew in defeat and humiliation. It was the beginning of the end of the Soviet Union. While many in the West believed the 'evil empire' had been vanquished by Ronald Reagan and Margaret Thatcher—with a little help from Gorbachev—Afghanistan's holy warriors believed *they* had defeated the Soviets. They saw the triumph of Islam over atheistic communism as proof that the superpowers were paper tigers.

Abdullah Anas, the young Algerian who had left home scarcely knowing where Afghanistan was on the map, witnessed the Soviet withdrawal from a vantage point high up in the Hindu Kush mountains. 'At that moment,' he told me later, his eyes shining bright with the memory, 'I knew that Allah keeps his promises.'[23]

* * *

The consequences for all concerned in the Afghan conflict were significant and in most cases ruinous. The war mortally wounded the Soviet Union, left Afghanistan ravaged and of no further interest to the Cold War protagonists, and served to Islamise Pakistan and its political culture in ways that have proved hard to reverse. Above all, the conflict gave birth to Al-Qaeda and set it on the road to 9/11.

In Afghanistan itself the aftermath of the war was chaotic. The quarrelling *mujahidin* factions turned on one another, precipitating a civil war which paved the way for the rise of the Taliban—the student movement sponsored by Pakistan and trained in its *madrasas*—which Afghans initially welcomed as an antidote to disorder, then progressively resented as it imposed its harsh rule on the country between 1996 and 2001.

Years later in Washington, I asked Bruce Riedel, who lived through the Afghan conflict during a thirty-year career with the CIA, whether it had all been worth it. Hadn't the United States unwittingly helped create a monster? His answer was two-fold. 'I think the war against the Soviet Union in Afghanistan was the right thing to do, and not just in terms of the geopolitics of the region—the Afghans did not want to be occupied by the Soviet Union.' But, yes, mistakes had been made. 'The error was in the aftermath—the period after 1989 when we put so little emphasis, and so little resources, not just in trying to find a solution to the Afghan civil war but in trying to build a Pakistan that could be stable and democratic.' Significantly, for most of the war, 'no one—including the CIA—thought these guys [the *mujahidin*] were going to win'. So the mistake had been to wake up to the danger too late, and then ignore Afghanistan once the Soviet forces had disengaged and it was no longer a Cold War battle.[24]

In the aftermath of the war Pakistan experienced a decade of civilian rule, with Benazir Bhutto and Nawaz Sharif alternating as prime minister. This ended abruptly in October 1999, when the army chief of staff General Pervez Musharraf seized power in the country's fourth military intervention. He made himself president in June 2001, a few months before the fateful attacks of 9/11. This was an especially traumatic moment for Pakistan. Under intense pressure from his ally, the United States, the general publicly broke with the Taliban, declaring himself a loyal partner of the Bush administration in its 'war on terror'. But following the US invasion of Afghanistan in 2001 and the overthrow of the Taliban, Pakistani policy became distinctly more ambiguous. The military were reluctant to sever their ties with Islamic militant groups—in Pakistan, in Kashmir, in Afghanistan—which they continued to find useful, obsessed as they were with the balance of power with India. Uprooting the culture of *jihad* was clearly going to be no easy task.

***

A few months after 9/11, I met a group of young Pakistanis in Lahore, all in their early twenties and supporters of *jihad*. These were, ideologically, Zia's children. They agreed to be interviewed on condition that I did not use their names. One admitted to having been 'up north', a euphemism for Kashmir. 'Holy war, or *jihad*,' he told me, 'is being done when you are being killed and your brothers and sisters are being killed innocently. This is not terrorism—this is to stop terrorism. I strongly believe that *jihad* will never be stopped,' he continued. 'The Prophet, peace be upon him, said that *jihad* will continue until the Day of Judgement.'[25]

These young men admired the Taliban and were angry that President Musharraf had switched sides. They were also angry at the pictures they saw every day on television—on CNN, Fox and the BBC—showing Israeli troops in action in the West Bank towns of Bethlehem and Jenin. So when I asked them who was to blame for the weakness of the Muslim world, I expected to hear the familiar litany of Western crimes against Islam. Instead they offered a very different explanation. 'We ourselves are to blame,' one of the young men replied, 'because we have not practised Islam in the right way. What Pakistan is doing and what the fifty-five or fifty-six Islamic countries are doing is not Islam. If we practise Islam in the right way, then nobody should be misbehaving with us in Jenin or Bethlehem. When we Muslims are united, everyone will respect us.'

This is the simple and seductive message of Salafism, the purist form of Sunni Islam usually associated with Saudi Arabia. The Salafis argue that the cause of Muslims' misfortunes is internal: they have strayed from the right path and only if they return to it will they become strong again.

But behind the apparent commitment of these young men, I detected a nagging uncertainty. In the course of a long conversation—much of it with the tape recorder switched off—one of them suddenly asked me if I thought Bin Laden had really carried out the attacks of 9/11. (Many Muslims at the time were in denial, preferring to believe the various conspiracy theories that were circulating.) I said I was in no doubt he had. 'If he *was* responsible,' said the young man despondently, 'he bears a heavy responsibility for what he has done to the Muslims.' The meaning was clear: because of 9/11, Muslims everywhere were under intense pressure; they themselves, as Pakistanis with militant sympathies, lived in constant fear of the knock on the door at night. It intrigued me that they were ready to entertain the possibility that their erstwhile hero had put them in such difficulty.

* * *

During my visit in 2002 I heard sharply contrasting views of Zia's legacy. For Pakistan's beleaguered liberals, it was poisonous. His notorious *hudud* ordinances were still on the statute book, even though they were seldom carried out. Hence a woman who had been raped could be convicted of adultery and, in theory, stoned to death. (In practice, the requirement of four witnesses to the act of penetration is virtually impossible to meet.) What lay behind such a legal culture? In the view of Tahira Abdullah, a tireless advocate of women's rights, 'a lethal mix of patriarchy, feudalism, tribalism, poverty—and a mindset that belies the trappings of modernity'. (In 2006 Musharraf issued a new law—the Protection of Women Act—which sought to curb some of the excesses of the *hudud* laws, but many Pakistani lawyers and human-rights activists felt it failed to go far enough.)[26]

Suroosh Irfani, writer, lecturer and Sufi intellectual, told me he saw a direct link between the religious violence of the jihadists and a collective loss of confidence rooted in colonial times. 'We haven't been able to shake off the legacy of colonisation—the downgrading of the individual—and that haunts us. And the haunting may be at the unconscious level: it has perhaps poisoned the Muslim subjectivity to the extent that there is this loss of confidence, this feeling that one is not good enough. And the flip-side of this loss of confidence, this passivity, is religious violence.'[27]

I heard a very different view from Hamid Gul, who regarded *jihad*—in its full-blooded sense—as a religious duty which no one, including Musharraf, could stop Muslims performing. He was outspokenly critical of the West's policies in the 'war on terror' and its efforts to badger Pakistan to take tougher action against Islamic militants. At the end of a wide-ranging interview, I asked him to set out his vision of the ideal Islamic state. It was as if I had touched a button and the floodgates had opened. 'There will be justice across the board,' he declared. 'The courts will be free: they will be interpreting the Qur'an, and it will put all anxieties at rest. Number two, the education system will be equal, not class-based—right now it is class-based—and *madrasas* will automatically disappear; but so will some of the public schools [which] are accessible only to the rich and mighty.

'The economic system will change,' he went on. 'There will be interest-free banking. The taxation will be direct—there will be no indirect taxation. And minorities will be free to practise their religion, their way of life, their culture—whatever they wish to. And feudalism will be no more [Gul chuckled]—that I can assure you. In Islam there is no place for feudalism. It says, "Land to the tillers." And, incidentally, the clerics will have no place, because Islam is not for the clerics. The clerics can appear before the court and give their point of view—but, beyond that, if they create bigotry and divide the society there is no place for them.

'And of course Pakistan will be a perfect democracy, because the sovereignty of Allah has to be practised through the people of Pakistan. There is no room for dictatorship, there is no room for usurpers, there is no room for people who want to perpetuate their own vested interest; none whatsoever.'[28]

Justice, education, democracy: it was a seductive vision and one with distinct echoes of Maududi's. But this was the man who had told the journalist Arnaud de Borchgrave that the 9/11 attacks were the work of Israeli intelligence, and who had spelt out rather more revealingly what the 'sovereignty of Allah' would entail: 'Democracy does not work. Politicians are constantly thinking of their next election, not the public good … The Qur'an calls a spade a spade. It is the supreme law and tells right from wrong. There is no notion of "my country right or wrong" under divine law. The creator's will predominates. All is subservient to Allah's will … The Prophet's last sermon was a universal document of human rights for everyone that surpasses everything that came since, including America's declaration of independence and the UN Charter ... divine law should supersede man-made law.'[29]

Gul had clearly retained his radical Islamist sympathies. In January 2001, together with other senior retired Pakistani military officers, he had taken part in a conference of some 300 Islamist figures in Peshawar. They had pledged loyalty to the Taliban and Bin Laden, whom they described as a 'great Muslim warrior'.[30]

So is Gul typical of the Pakistani officer class? It is sometimes suggested that the army is a hotbed of religious fervour. What is often overlooked is that many of the military men who supported (and in some cases still support) Zia's policies did so out of patriotism rather than religious zeal. Even Pervez Musharraf, a member of the secular, whiskey-drinking wing of the military, essentially shared Zia's view of the utility of *jihad*. As Steve Coll puts it, 'For Musharraf, as for many other liberal Pakistani generals, *jihad* was not a calling, it was a professional imperative. It was something he did at the office.'[31] Zia himself, for all his commitment to Islamisation, was no wild-eyed fanatic, but a shrewd soldier-politician who used religion for calculated ends.

A distinguished historian of the Pakistani military, Shuja Nawaz, observes that: 'While the army remains a conservative institution at heart, it is not yet a breeding ground for large numbers of radical Islamists that many fear.' His verdict nevertheless on the Zia years and their legacy is unsparing: 'His régime was to be the longest military rule in Pakistan's history with far-reaching effects that still haunt the body politic of Pakistan. It witnessed ... the rise of Islamists in the military, and state sponsorship of militant Islamic (largely Sunni) sectarian groups (which provoked a Shia backlash and spawned sectarian warfare).'

The Zia era, he adds, 'also saw the maturation of the country's nuclear technology, the intrusion of the military into almost all sectors of the economy, and a growing Culture of Entitlement, reflected in state-endorsed asset accumulation and corruption, in both the civil and military environment. The resulting stunting of political activity and discourse left the country teetering after Zia's sudden departure from the scene.'[32]

Pakistan is now widely regarded as the most dangerous country in the world. The root cause of its predicament is that Jinnah's vision of a Muslim renaissance in the Indian subcontinent was subverted by the culture of *jihad* which Zia, Gul and their foreign patrons nurtured in the 1980s.

4

A BRIDGE TO AFRICA

An old taxi with a cracked windscreen drove me to Friendship Hall beside the Nile in Khartoum. The hall, built by the Chinese in the 1970s, would over the next few days be the scene of a performance of political theatre devised by the *eminence grise* of Sudanese politics, Hasan al-Turabi.

I had reached Khartoum, after a difficult ten-hour journey from London via Amsterdam and Cairo, at three o'clock that morning. There was no bank open at the airport, so I had no Sudanese money. A taxi took me to the Acropole Hotel, much beloved by budget-conscious NGOs, where the driver asked me for 5,000 dinars (about $10). Asking him to wait, I climbed the stairs to the first floor of the hotel and woke up the night-time receptionist, who was asleep on a sofa. Yes, he had my reservation; but no, he was not allowed to change money. I went back down, offered my business card to the taxi driver and asked him if he would mind coming back later when the banks were open. He did. As I turned to go back into the hotel, he was still gesticulating grumpily.

Khartoum in the spring of 1995 was, at first glance, straight out of a Graham Greene novel. Battered yellow taxis creaked and groaned as they navigated streets full of dust, rubbish and potholes. The fabled Blue Nile was brown and languid. The Acropole was friendly but, well, basic. Phones worked erratically. This was, in short, a big, poor African country of some twenty-five million people. Yet since Turabi and his National Islamic Front—the Sudanese wing of the Muslim Brotherhood—had seized power in a military coup in 1989, it had been the unlikely setting for an Islamic revolution.

I had come to attend the Popular Arab and Islamic Conference, which Turabi had hosted in Khartoum since 1991. The event epitomised the new Islamism, bringing together the voices of Muslim dissent not just from the Middle East but from all over the world. By the 1990s Islamism had been internationalised by the twin phenomena of the Khomeini revolution in Iran and the anti–Soviet war in Afghanistan. Khartoum had become a hub on the global Islamist map.[1]

Sudan is unpromising material for Islamic revolution. It sits on the fault-line between the Muslim Arab world and non-Muslim black Africa, and a civil war between north and south has continued almost uninterrupted since independence from Britain in the 1950s. But the revolutionaries, undeterred, had set out to 'Islamise' Sudanese society whether it liked it or not. Military men held the top positions, with Turabi playing the role of 'guide', rather as Khomeini had done in Iran, ostensibly aloof from politics. But, revealingly, when Western diplomats in Khartoum wanted to get something done, it was to Turabi that they turned.

For anyone expecting a traditional Muslim society where women had a low profile, there were some surprises in store. In Sudan these days, a businessman told me with a slightly rueful grin, the women were running the show. A feature of Turabi's ostensibly progressive Islam was his view that women should play an active role in public life. 'Women in Sudan are free,' his wife Wisal al-Mahdi told me when we met during the conference—free to dress as they wanted, free to be active in civil society, free to stand for parliament. There were twenty-five women MPs, she told me proudly—twenty Muslims and five Christians.

The notion that women were free was, as I later discovered, not true. But, at first glance, women *were* now active in politics and the professions and in the universities—even in the police and the armed forces. I went to see Sumaya Abu-Khashawa, an energetic geneticist who ran the General Union of Sudanese Women. The union had three priorities, she told me: education, including literacy classes; income-generating programmes for women; and political mobilisation. The union was committed to making women aware of 'how they can have more share in society and in decision-making'.

But, as I learned from a United Nations official, the development challenges were formidable. In 1995 the largest country in Africa—a quarter the size of Europe—had less than 500 miles of paved roads. Healthcare was patchy, with malaria the biggest killer. Only seventeen per cent of women were literate, as opposed to forty-three per cent of men. Rural women married, on average, at seventeen; urban women at twenty. Female circumcision was still common: the government, over-zealously, had pledged to eradicate it by the year 2000.

In the eyes of the government's critics, it was mobilising women for its own narrow purposes. It was an unelected régime that had to drum up support where it could. Moreover some women were decidedly more equal than others. Back in London I had visited a group of Sudanese exiles with grim stories to tell of the régime's excesses. They included Mona Khujali, one of the many educated women who had been forced to flee the country since the Islamist takeover. She summed up the six–year rule of Turabi and his National Islamic Front as 'six years of torture, imprisonment, disappearances, killing, executions and war'. Women who objected to the régime's policies had been dismissed from their jobs, imprisoned, flogged in the streets. 'Only women who belong to the Islamic Front,' she declared dismissively, 'are able to do whatever they want.'[2]

* * *

The Arabs called it *bilad al-sudan*, the land of the blacks. As a country straddling black Africa and the Arab world, Sudan's relationship with its neighbours to the north has always been ambivalent. If the Arabs gave Sudan Islam, the Arabic language and Arab brotherhood, they also gave it slavery and misrule. In 1820 Muhammad Ali—the modernising ruler of Egypt we encountered in Chapter One—sent a force led by his son Ismail to invade and conquer Sudan. Since he was acting, nominally at least, in the name of the Ottoman empire, this period, which lasted until 1881, is known in Sudanese history as the Turkiyah. The people of the *bilad al-sudan* resented Turco-Egyptian rule, which they regarded as repressive and exploitative. One of Muhammad Ali's motives was to control the slave trade and conscript black (non-Muslim) slaves into his army. 'The slave trade quickly grew in volume and intensified in brutality ... Within a year 30,000 Sudanese slaves were sent to Egypt for training and induction into [Muhammad Ali's] army, but so many perished from disease and an unfamiliar climate that they could be used effectively only in garrisons in Sudan.'[3]

By the 1880s Britain was playing a dominant role in Egypt's affairs, and was increasingly becoming entangled in Sudan's, too. After six decades of the Turkiyah, resentment of foreign interference gave birth to an Islamic revivalist movement which served as a historical precedent for Turabi's revolution. In 1881 Muhammad Ahmad—known to history as the Mahdi—launched a holy war to impose Islamic law and drive out the foreigners (which meant the Turks and the Egyptians no less than the British). The Mahdi soon gained in prestige and military strength. The Turkiyah gave way to the Mahdiyah, which the Sudanese regard with pride as 'the only successful anti–imperialist Islamic republic in Africa at the time'.[4]

The British authorities were at first unwilling to take on the Mahdi. Instead they sent General Charles Gordon to evacuate the Egyptians from Khartoum. The Mahdi's forces—the Ansar, some 30,000–strong—laid siege to the city for almost a year. Then in 1885 they stormed it, killing Gordon. The Mahdi died a few months later, but his Islamic state survived for a dozen more years until 1898, when a British and Egyptian force under General Kitchener defeated the Ansar and avenged the death of 'Gordon of Khartoum'.

For the next half-century Sudan was officially under joint British and Egyptian rule but was in fact a British colony in all but name. Since many of those recruited by the British to run the country were sportsmen from Oxford and Cambridge, wags referred to the Sudanese as 'blacks ruled by blues'.[5] In 1956 Sudan finally became independent, the first sub-Saharan African country to do so. But its post-colonial history has witnessed a constant alternation of military and civilian rule, with coups in 1958 and 1969 and finally the seizure of power by army officers in June 1989.

The ideological tendency of the plotters, led by Brigadier General Omar al-Bashir, was not at first apparent. But it subsequently became clear that the timing of the coup was designed to thwart a peace agreement in the south to which they were strongly opposed. In 1990 General Bashir declared Sudan an Islamic state, and the new régime sought to enforce its own interpretation of Islamic law. Alcohol was banned, and violators received forty lashes. Women in government offices, schools and universities were told to cover their heads. The Islamists set out to weaken the Sufi brotherhoods which had traditionally enjoyed a large grass-roots following in the country and in some cases considerable political influence. They sought to 'recapture the allegedly more authentic traditions of Islam in Sudan' which had 'become overlain and corrupted with the superstitions and other-worldliness of Sufism'.[6]

Political parties and trade unions were banned. Key institutions—the army, the civil service, the judiciary and the universities—were purged. Attempted coups were ruthlessly crushed. The press was brought under control. Dissent was repressed, with well-documented use of arbitrary detention, torture and even death. An alternative army was created—the 150,000–strong Popular Defence Forces—in which civil servants and university students had to undergo three months of compulsory training, after which many of them became cannon-fodder for the war in the south. The régime saw the south as not merely non-Muslim but, as a result of the activities of Christian missionaries, anti–Muslim. It set out to rescue the southerners in the name of the true faith.

In 1991 the country formally aligned itself with the Islamic Republic of Iran, which shared Turabi's hope that it could serve as a bridge to bring Islamism from the Middle East to Africa. The new relationship was sealed in a visit to Sudan in December 1991 by the Iranian president, Akbar Hashemi Rafsanjani. He brought with him 157 officials, including five government ministers and the head of the Revolutionary Guard. Addressing a mass wedding in Khartoum for more than a thousand couples, he praised the country's 'revolutionary adherence to Islam'. Iran agreed to supply Sudan with oil and underwrite its arms purchases from China.[7]

***

The 1990s witnessed an upsurge of political Islam in Arab Africa. While in the continent's largest country the Islamists had seized power on the back of a military coup, in Algeria, the second largest, they came within a whisker of winning it through the ballot-box. The rise and fall of the Algerian opposition party the FIS, or Islamic Salvation Front, is a salutary tale of how the ascent to power of a populist grass-roots Islamist movement was thwarted by military men who saw themselves as saviours of the nation.

The French had occupied Algeria in 1830 and ruled it for a hundred and thirty-two years. Unlike the British in Egypt or Sudan, the colonial power had encouraged large numbers of Europeans to settle as farmers, shopkeepers and administrators. By 1886 there were 430,000 settlers (or *pieds noirs*, as they came to be called) and by 1954 almost a million, living among eight million Arabs. Among them was the novelist Albert Camus, whose last, posthumously published book, *The First Man*, is a vivid picture of the life of an impoverished European family in Algiers. The settlers knew how to pull strings in Paris and were determined to keep alive the notion that Algeria was an integral part of France. This helps explain the bitterness and bloodshed of the Algerian war of independence, which broke out in 1954, lasted nearly eight years and, according to a leading historian of French colonialism, cost some half a million lives.[8]

At independence in 1962, the country was physically and psychologically ravaged. Only fifteen per cent of a predominantly rural population were literate. The movement which had won the country's freedom, the National Liberation Front, or FLN, believed it was entitled to govern unopposed. But in fact the fierce in-fighting that had characterised its conduct of the war of liberation was carried over into the post-colonial period. The dominant figure from 1965 until his death in 1978, and the man who did most to shape the character of independent Algeria, was the austere, secretive Colonel Houari Boumediène. Boumediène used the country's considerable oil and gas revenues to implement an unwritten social contract with the people: the ruling FLN would (in theory at least) provide jobs and houses and education, and in return the Algerians would accept the dictates of an authoritarian system which allowed little room for pluralism or dissent.

When I first visited Algeria in 1977 a young official told me confidently that the country was creating its own blend of Marx and Muhammad. Boumediène was an avowed socialist and an ally of the Soviet Union, and his mission was to build a top-heavy Soviet-style command economy. But at the same time he saw a role for Islam in nation-building—provided it was an Islam firmly under the state's control. After more than a decade in power, he still enjoyed a certain respect among ordinary people because of his personal incorruptibility and his championing of social justice at home and a New World Order abroad. Algerians felt they counted for something in the world. But there were already signs that the social contract was fraying. The population had swollen to seventeen million, almost half of whom were under fifteen. As I travelled by bus from the coastal plain, where most of the population is concentrated, to the Saharan interior, *hittistes*—young men propping up walls—were everywhere to be seen. Many were unemployed. In the over-crowded apartment blocks of Algiers it was not uncommon to find a family of ten living in a single room. The seeds of future trouble were there, though I scarcely realised it at the time.

It was only after Boumediène's death from a rare blood disease at the age of fifty-three, and the succession of another colonel, Chadli Benjedid, that things began to fall apart. Chadli lacked his predecessor's prestige. He initially benefited from a petrodollar windfall, but this abruptly ended with the oil-price collapse of the mid-1980s. Unemployment and the cost of living soared. The housing shortage became even more acute. By 1987 the population had grown to twenty-three million. As the state was no longer fulfilling its side of the bargain, a growing number of Algerians began to call into question its legitimacy; and some did so using the language of Islam. Social and economic grievances exploded in the popular protests of October 1988, during which the army fired on predominantly youthful demonstrators, leaving as many as five hundred dead.[9] The Algerian *intifada* was a turning-point which led Chadli to embark on an unprecedented opening-up of a stagnant political system. The FLN's quarter of a century of power was about to end.

Chadli saw himself as an Arab Gorbachev. He courted the West, especially France, and opened up the economy. The term 'Algerian socialism', omnipresent since 1962, 'disappeared overnight'.[10] In initiating multi–party politics, he calculated he could use political Islam to buttress his legitimacy and weaken his opponents on the left. Ahead of local elections in 1990, a dozen new political parties sprang up, the most significant of which was the Islamist party, the FIS. In the event the FIS won almost twice as many votes as the FLN. Buoyed by this success, the FIS leaders, Ali Belhadj and Abbassi Madani, pressed for parliamentary elections, to which Chadli finally agreed. The run-up to the elections was stormy. The FIS opted for mass protest, calling an 'unlimited' strike. Many in the régime and in the military began to panic. Madani and Belhadj were arrested. It was in this climate of tension that the first round of elections took place in December 1991. To the consternation of Algerian liberals, leftists and secular feminists—and to the fury of many in the army and the FLN who regarded Chadli's democratic experiment as the height of recklessness—almost half of those who took part (47%) voted for the FIS. It was a flawed election but it showed unmistakably that the FIS was 'the single strongest political movement in the country'.[11]

In one of the most traumatic moments in the story of the Muslim revolt, the army intervened, cancelled the second round of elections, removed Chadli from power and outlawed the FIS. The Algerian experience offered no end of a lesson. To the governments of the region, disaster had only narrowly been averted. The moral was that if you heeded the promptings of the West and embarked on democratisation, the Islamists would sweep you from power. Not surprisingly, Islamists drew a rather different conclusion. Moderate Islamism was a cul-de-sac: as soon as they got close to power via the ballot-box, the rules of the game were changed and they were disqualified. In their eyes, the FIS became a kind of martyred movement and proof that Western talk of democracy was humbug.

In Algeria itself, the Islamist movement—never monolithic—split into fragments. Throughout the 1990s, a brutal war was waged between the military-backed régime and a variety of armed Islamic groups in which anywhere between 100,000 and 200,000 Algerians were killed.

* * *

By the mid-1990s, the Islamist movements and the Arab régimes had reached an impasse. In Egypt, the security forces were cracking down hard on violent Islamist groups (offshoots of the Muslim Brotherhood), but proved unable to eradicate Islamism as a political force. In the Palestinian territories, Yasser Arafat's ruling nationalist faction, Fatah, was coming under growing pressure from Hamas, the Islamist movement born in Gaza in the late 1980s during the first *intifada* (uprising) against Israeli occupation. And in Algeria there was no end in sight to the bloody insurrection. In all of these places, Hasan al-Turabi was supporting the Islamist opposition against the governing authority, which made him a hate figure among Western-backed Middle East leaders, as well as in the West.

Turabi had hosted the first Popular Arab and Islamic Conference in Khartoum in April 1991. Its birth was a response to the Gulf war, a few months before, in which a Western-led coalition had expelled Saddam Hussein's forces from Kuwait. The war split the Arab world into pro-American and anti–American camps, and Turabi wanted to mobilise the anti–American forces under the banner of Islam. Some 200 representatives from forty-five countries attended the conference, together with 300 Sudanese. Turabi was chosen as secretary-general. The choice of the terms 'Arab' and 'Islamic' in the conference's name showed his pragmatism: he wanted to ride the two horses of Arabism and Islamism, rather than abandoning the one for the sake of the other. The event was funded by private donors and also, it was whispered, by Iran.[12]

The conference I attended in 1995 was the third. From Turabi's point of view, the forum had several purposes. It enabled Muslim groups from around the world to meet and to network; it put Sudan on the map; and at the same time it gave him a bigger stage on which to perform, as the leader not merely of a large, poor African country but of a transnational movement which, he was convinced, was becoming a force to be reckoned with.

I looked around the conference hall where, according to one of the Sudanese organisers, eighty countries were represented. I could see an exiled member of the FIS, Hamas activists from Palestine, a firebrand sheikh from Yemen, Muslim Brothers (and the occasional sister) from Egypt and Jordan, activists from Turkey, Iran and Central Asia, and black American Muslims from Louis Farrakhan's Nation of Islam. Neatly dressed as ever, in jacket and tie, the retired Pakistani general Hamid Gul denounced Indian 'imperialism' in Kashmir. The basis of the Western nation-state, he declared, was secularism—and the Western nation-state was crumbling. A British Muslim convert attacked the interest-based international banking system, declaring that the letters IMF stood for 'intimidation, murder and fraud'.

But the star of the show was Turabi himself who, in turban and flowing white robe, delivered a high-voltage speech in Arabic. Young female cheerleaders began chanting as he stood up to address the conference, and egged him on as he hit the popular buttons of Palestine, the aggression and dishonesty of the West and the abject failure of the Arab régimes, which even now, he declared, were cowering in the face of a popular Muslim revolt. The West and its allies wanted democracy, but only for themselves. 'Democracy must even be buried alive at infancy,' he declared, in an obvious reference to Algeria, 'lest it assume an Islamic character.' Without naming names, he attacked those 'Muslims who bend to appease the West ... in betrayal of their own people'. Turning to Muslim communities in the West, he called Bosnia 'the gaping wound in the side of the Muslim world, and the playground for Western hypocrisy'. This was the hot gospel of the new Islamism, and the audience loved it.

Three days later, at the end of the conference, Turabi held a press conference on the fourth floor of Friendship Hall to read a draft of the final declaration. It called on Muslim countries to reject normalisation of relations with Israel and to support armed struggle against the Jewish state. It called for an 'Islamic United Nations', but at the same time supported efforts to open a Muslim dialogue with the West. After some debate, the conference had voted to drop the word 'Arab' from its title; the Arab nationalists had been out-voted.

At six o'clock there was a break for evening prayers, and then, in the question-and-answer session with the media, Turabi came into his own. Moving easily between Arabic and English, he insisted this had been a 'conference of moderates'.

He claimed that Amnesty International—which had produced a new report on Sudan's egregious human-rights abuses—was in the pay of British intelligence. He mocked Yasser Arafat for being the mayor of Gaza. He asserted that the Sudanese government had not paid a single dinar towards the cost of the conference, but was vague about where the money had come from.

When I visited Turabi in his office the next day, where he had agreed to give me an interview, I found him relaxed and fluent and hard to pin down. He projected the image of the ideologue of the revolution rather than its chief executive. He wanted visitors to know that he was well read and well travelled; he could criticise the West with authority because he had lived there and knew its ways. Turabi was then sixty-three, his neatly-trimmed beard flecked with white. He had been born in 1932, during colonial rule, into a family known for its piety. His father was a Muslim judge who worked in the Shari'a courts set up by the British to deal with matters of personal status. Turabi's political activism began in 1950, when he went to study law at the University of Khartoum—one of Africa's oldest (founded in 1902) and then a hotbed of rivalry between communists, nationalists and Islamists. This was the period when the ideology of the Muslim Brotherhood, transplanted from its native Egypt, was taking root in Sudan.

After graduating, Turabi left for Europe, where he continued his legal studies at the London School of Economics and the Sorbonne. Returning home in 1964, now in his early thirties, he immediately plunged back into Islamist politics. By the late 1960s he had become 'the most visible and influential figure in the Islamic movement in Sudan'.[13] Like many Islamists, Turabi was influenced by the seminal figures of Al-Banna and Maududi, but he followed his own path. He was convinced Muslim intellectuals had a central role to play in working out how to apply

Islamic principles in modern societies. He was dismissive of official *ulama* (religious scholars) and did not follow any one school of Islamic law.[14]

Sitting in his office dressed in a white turban and a white robe, with an elegant scarf draped round his neck, Turabi talked proudly of Sudan's 'social revolution' and of how women were no longer tied to the home. He contrasted his own all-embracing view of religion with the West's futile attempts to put God in a box. 'It's so irrational,' he said, 'to believe that God is only inside the church or inside the mosque—[that] I worship him there and then I lock him up. If there is a God, he's omnipresent—present everywhere—and he's omnipotent. So this Western idea of God is unintelligible.'

As he spoke and chuckled and those dazzling teeth flashed, one succumbed for a moment to the charm and wit. Only when he described as a *jihad* the long-running Sudanese civil war did one sense the hard ideological edge. When I asked whether Sudan was playing host to training camps for foreign Muslims—something that troubled Western diplomats in Khartoum—he issued the standard denial. Sudan gave hospitality to fellow Arabs and fellow Muslims; but lurid Western reports of training camps in the desert were pure fantasy.

Even as he spoke, there hovered on the fringes of the conference a tall young Arabian called Osama.

Faisaliah—built by rival princely families. Around it is a complex of smart shops (Debenhams, Harvey Nichols, Marks & Spencer) where wealthy Saudi women buy clothes. This is the Oxford Street of Riyadh.

Eye-witnesses told me what had happened. Hundreds of Saudi demonstrators had gathered near the tower that afternoon—perhaps as many as 500, though officials spoke later of less than half that number. They had called for political reform and the release of political prisoners. There had been men with beards chanting 'God is great', a small number of women holding up photos of their imprisoned relatives and a lot of *shabab* (young men). The police had been taken by surprise. After more than an hour, they arrested dozens of demonstrators, including some of the women, and dispersed the rest.

The shock of the event was palpable. One young Saudi official told me Riyadh had never seen anything like it. A newspaper the following morning quoted a leading pro-government cleric as denouncing the demonstration as 'the behaviour of non-Muslims'. The authorities were embarrassed that such an event could occur in the centre of their capital. The timing as well as the location of the protest had been cleverly chosen: it coincided with the country's first human-rights conference, which had drawn diplomats, lawyers and journalists from around the world. The authorities were also stung by the fact that the call for the demonstration had come from a well-known Saudi dissident in London, Saad al-Faqih, using a radio station and phone-in programme broadcast from Europe.

These were dark days for Saudi Arabia. Not only was it under the harsh glare of international attention after the 9/11 attacks against New York and Washington, most of whose perpetrators had been Saudi. A few months before the demonstration, in May 2003. Al-Qaeda had launched a campaign of violence in the kingdom with a string of suicide bombings of residential compounds in Riyadh. One way or another, Islamist dissent had arrived with a vengeance.[1]

* * *

Saudi Arabia is, on the face of it, an unlikely theatre of Muslim revolt. The Arabian peninsula is the cradle of Islam, the site of its most revered holy places (Mecca and Medina) and the birthplace of its Prophet. What's more, the basis of the modern Saudi state is an eighteenth-century alliance between a religious scholar, Muhammad Ibn Abdel-Wahhab, and a tribal dynasty, the House of Saud. Ibn Abdel-Wahhab was the founder of the austere form of Sunni Islam—usually known as Wahhabism—which is the *raison d'être* of the Saudi state.

I went out one day to the ruins of the old capital, Dir'iyah, a short drive from Riyadh. Proud of their ancestral home, the Al-Saud are pouring millions of dollars into its restoration. Here, amid the noise of trucks and bulldozers, I walked in the shell of the mosque where the founder of Wahhabism had preached. With me was the Saudi scholar Ahmad Turkistani. We talked about the significance of that historic alliance forged more than two and a half centuries ago.[2] For the Al-Saud the alliance provided legitimacy, and Wahhabism became the instrument for the expansion of their power. For Muhammad Ibn Abdel-Wahhab, it was the basis for a campaign to purify the practice of Islam in the land of the Prophet, which he believed had fallen into corruption and decay. He accused the Muslims of Arabia of worshipping trees and stones and the tombs of saints, which in his eyes was the intolerable sin of *shirk* (idolatry). He advocated a strict monotheism: the core of his belief was *tawhid*, the oneness and indivisibility of Allah.

Ibn Abdel-Wahhab was clear about what Wahhabism rejected. In the words of a Western scholar, 'It rejected the corruption and laxity of the contemporary decline. It rejected too the accommodations and cultural richness of the medieval [Islamic] empire. It rejected the introvert warmth and other-worldly piety of the mystic way. It rejected also the alien intellectualism not only of philosophy but of theology. It rejected all dissensions, even the now well-established Shi'ah. It insisted solely on the Law.'[3]

As a consequence, Wahhabism has a reputation for intolerance. It was from the start contested; even Ibn Abdel-Wahhab's brother opposed it. And because the word itself was (and is) used by critics as a term of abuse, Saudis themselves tend to avoid it. A prominent Saudi prince, Turki al-Faisal, told me, 'There is no such thing as Wahhabism. That's a canard that's meant to confuse, so that people can find something to blame.'[4] When I asked Professor Turkistani how he would describe himself, he replied: 'We are the followers of the reform movement of Muhammad Ibn Abdel-Wahhab.' Others prefer to call themselves Salafis. Salafis draw their inspiration from the pious ancestors (al-salaf al-salih), the early generations of Muslims who were closest to the Prophet and his message. Salafism is an older and broader movement than Wahhabism. One of its most important ideologues is the revered medieval scholar Ibn Taymiyya (1263–1328), whose writings constituted 'a monumental effort to purge Islamic belief of what he considered to be accumulated heresies and to refute these in a systematic manner'.[5] He sought to strip away un-Islamic innovation (bid'a) and restore the pristine Islam of the Prophet's day. Salafis favour extreme textual literalism, reject the authority of the four traditional schools of law in Sunni Islam and are ready to engage in excommunication (takfir) of Muslims who flout what they deem to be Islamic norms. Although Wahhabism and Salafism are not synonymous, they are kindred spirits and over time Salafism has become closely associated with the Saudi religious establishment.

The modern Saudi state was created in 1932 by Abdel-Aziz al-Saud, the country's founder and first king, better known in the West as Ibn Saud. The historian Elizabeth Monroe singled him out as one of the six leading figures in the making of the modern Middle East.[6] In the first three decades of the twentieth century, Abdel-Aziz carved out the new state from the greater part of the Arabian peninsula. Had imperial Britain not set the limits to Saudi expansion, in deference to the smaller Gulf sheikhdoms with which it had relations, his kingdom would have been bigger still. Even so, it is four times the size of France.

Abdel-Aziz needed a powerful foreign protector. In the period before the modern kingdom was created this was Britain, and from the 1930s, when oil was first discovered, and increasingly after the Second World War, it became the United States. Gradually a close political, economic and military alliance with Washington was formed. The implicit bargain on which it is built, based on America's need for oil and the Al-Saud's for security, has proved remarkably resilient.

I sought out two people, a Saudi and a Briton, who knew Abdel-Aziz in his old age. The Saudi businessman Suleiman Olayan dealt with the king in the early days of oil, and remembers a tall, imposing man who conducted his relations shrewdly with the two big Western powers of the time. Why had he given the Americans, not the British, the first oil concession in 1933? Because America had no colonial baggage. Although still dependent on the British, Abdel-Aziz mistrusted them. For his part, the British diplomat Sir Philip Adams, who spent two years in Saudi Arabia from 1945, heard the old king tell stories of his battles, as he delighted in doing. This could be unnerving. On one occasion, as the king was describing how he had charged on camelback towards an adversary, he seized one of the swords displayed on the wall to show the startled young diplomat how he'd cut off the man's head and sent it rolling away in the sand.[7]

Abdel-Aziz unified the tribes of Arabia by conquest and intermarriage—in the Arab phrase, with a sword of steel and a sword of flesh. Having defeated a tribe he would bind it to him by marrying one of its women. (At his death he left more than thirty sons.) His warriors, the shock troops of Wahhabism, were known as the Ikhwan, or Brotherhood. The Ikhwan interpreted the injunction against *bid'a* to mean the banning of music, dancing, photography, tobacco, hashish and silk clothes. They were suspicious of the telephone, the telegraph and the automobile. When they conquered a town, they would smash luxuries, such as mirrors, for which they saw no need. Their actions also intensified the sense of mistrust among communities—such as the Shi'a of the Eastern Province and the Hijazis of the western coast—who eschewed the Wahhabi interpretation of Islam and felt (and still feel) threatened by it.

The Ikhwan were the instrument of Abdel-Aziz's success. But when they turned against him, chafing against his close ties to Britain and the limits he set on their raids, he crushed them. The state he created in 1932 was poor, backward and sparsely populated. Disease and illiteracy were rife. But after the Second World War, oil started to flow in significant quantities, under the direction of the American company Aramco. And all at once the flood of *bid'a*—innovations that conservative Wahhabis shunned—became unstoppable. A simple desert society was thrust into modernity. Roads and schools were built and modern medicine was introduced. By the time the one-eyed, battle-scarred old king died in 1953, modernisation, with its undreamt-of benefits and jarring dislocations, had begun to transform the desert kingdom.

* * *

On King Fahd Road, a busy highway in Riyadh, stands a modern building of concrete and glass bearing the name the World Assembly of Muslim Youth. WAMY is one of the best-known Saudi charities, active throughout the Muslim world, and I have come to see its head, Dr Saleh al-Wohaibi. He receives me courteously, but it's clear the charities are uncomfortable with the glare of publicity they've had to endure since 9/11. They stand accused of, wittingly or unwittingly, funding Al-Qaeda and the global *jihad*.[8]

WAMY is one of the pan-Islamic organisations created by King Faisal in the 1960s and 1970s. Since the death of its first king, Saudi Arabia has been ruled in turn by five of his sons—Saud, Faisal, Khalid, Fahd and Abdullah. The rule of the dissolute Saud was an unhappy interlude which split the ruling family and bankrupted the treasury. After a six–year struggle for power that the family has never forgotten, Saud was edged out in favour of his brother Faisal. Faisal was a frugal man who disliked princely profligacy. He lived in an unostentatious house and drove himself to the office every day. He was a moderniser, albeit a cautious one, who created a modern bureaucracy, organised the oil industry and brought the kingdom's finances under tighter control. In centralising power, he built a stronger, more pro-Western and more autocratic state, intolerant of dissent.

To counter what he saw as the twin threat of communism and Arab nationalism (championed by his regional rival President Nasser of Egypt), Faisal fashioned an Islamic foreign policy which the kingdom has pursued ever since. He had abundant means to do so: as a result of the oil embargo which accompanied the Arab-Israeli war of 1973, oil prices quadrupled. The king used the new flood of petrodollars to create a moderate bloc of Muslim states under Saudi tutelage, utilising the slogan of the solidarity of the *umma* (the worldwide community of the faithful). This involved building an infrastructure of institutions with a pan-Islamic purpose, including the Muslim World League (created in 1962), the Organisation of the Islamic Conference (1972), WAMY (1972) and the International Islamic Relief Organisation (1975). Over time, this infrastructure of Islamic institutions became strengthened and politicised.[9]

Faisal was shot dead in 1975 by an aggrieved nephew. He was succeeded by his brother Khalid, who showed little interest in governing the kingdom and left the affairs of state in the hands of Crown Prince Fahd. The late 1970s were a dangerous time for Saudi Arabia. A number of crises intersected in 1979, the year in which the Shah of Iran was overthrown and the Soviet Union blundered into Afghanistan. In retrospect, this was the geopolitical moment that gave birth to revolutionary Islamism, in both its Sunni and Shi'ite forms. The Saudi kingdom felt threatened from within and without. The fact that an apparently powerful American-backed ruler like the Shah could be overthrown in a popular revolution was deeply unsettling for the Saudi princes. What's more, his successor, Ayatollah Khomeini, lost no time in castigating them as stooges of America, unfit to guard the holy places of Mecca and Medina.

At home, the kingdom faced both Sunni and Shi'ite unrest. In November 1979 the Great Mosque in Mecca was seized by a group of Sunni Muslim insurgents, both Saudi and non-Saudi, who denounced the House of Saud as an 'infidel clique' and proclaimed the advent of the Mahdi, or messiah. Around the same time there was serious unrest among the kingdom's Shi'ite minority in the oil-rich Eastern Province. King Khalid and Crown Prince Fahd felt they had to bolster the régime in the face of these multiple challenges by strengthening and pouring money into the religious establishment, the *mutawa* (religious police) and a variety of other Islamic institutions. The individuals and groups who gained money and enhanced status were those who had emerged from the infrastructure built up by Faisal in his Islamisation of Saudi foreign policy.[10]

* * *

In that fateful year of 1979, a twenty-two-year-old Saudi called Osama bin Laden entered university in Jeddah. At a moment of extraordinary ferment in the Muslim world, when both superpowers found themselves entangled with a militant Islam that was rapidly becoming internationalised, the young Bin Laden experienced his political coming-of-age.

The outlines of his story are well known. Born in Riyadh in 1957, he was the son of a Yemeni migrant worker who had become a highly successful construction magnate in the Saudi kingdom, building roads, mosques and palaces for the House of Saud. One of the young Bin Laden's childhood friends remembers him as gentle and devout, a child of Wahhabism who had the quiet authority to influence his peers. When he enrolled to study business administration at King Abdel-Aziz University in Jeddah, it seemed likely his future lay in the family firm. Instead he came under the spell of two prominent figures in the Muslim Brotherhood. In the 1950s and 1960s, the kingdom had given refuge to members of the Brotherhood who had been jailed and persecuted by Nasser in Egypt or by other secular-nationalist régimes in the region. Many of these refugees became university teachers, among them Muhammad Qutb—the younger brother of Sayyid Qutb, the Islamist ideologue Nasser had hanged in 1966—and a charismatic Palestinian, Abdullah Azzam. Under their influence Bin Laden was recruited into the Brotherhood.[11]

The marriage of Wahhabism with the politics of the Muslim Brotherhood produced the movement known as the Sahwa al-Islamiya, or Islamic Awakening, to which many young Saudis

103

like Bin Laden were drawn. The movement came to be led by two charismatic young religious scholars, Safar al-Hawali and Salman al-Awda. They and their followers were impatient with conservative Wahhabis who believed that it was the duty of the rulers to rule and that scholars should not meddle in worldly affairs. This apolitical stance suited the ruling princes well, enabling them to co-opt a group of loyal *ulama* who legitimised their rule and refrained from commenting on their social vices and their close ties to an infidel power, the United States. With the Muslim world in such upheaval, many of the new generation of Saudis despised such subservience and sought a more active engagement in the politics of the Muslim *umma*.[12]

The followers of the Sahwa were not at first in confrontation with the state. On the contrary, the new policy of Khalid and Fahd enabled them to build up their presence in institutions such as the wealthy state-backed charities and the Islamic universities, both of which were ideal recruiting-grounds. Besides, on the foreign-policy issue of the day, the war in Afghanistan, the state and the Sahwa were at one. Young Saudis and other Arabs were encouraged by their governments to join the Afghan *jihad* against the communist oppressors. With the help of his mentor Abdullah Azzam, Bin Laden became one of the leaders of the 'Arab Afghans', using his wealth and charisma to motivate and organise a band of Arab *mujahidin* (holy warriors) from Saudi Arabia and elsewhere. There is little reason to believe their military contribution was significant, but, as we have seen, the episode nevertheless had fateful consequences. It was in the mountains of Afghanistan in the 1980s that a new generation of battle-hardened Sunni Islamists emerged to form the nucleus of Al-Qaeda.

Bin Laden was not yet a critic of the House of Saud, since for the time being he was its ally in the anti–communist cause. The turning-point—the moment when he and other

Saudi Islamists began to rebel against the state—was the Gulf war of 1990–91. Fahd, who was now king, saw Saddam Hussein's invasion of Kuwait in the summer of 1990 as a direct threat. After an anxious council of the senior princes, he invited US troops to defend the kingdom and use it as a launching-pad for the liberation of Kuwait. The presence of half-a-million infidel soldiers on the sacred soil of Arabia created a powerful backlash, incensing and radicalising the country's fledgling Islamist opposition movement. In a book called *Kissinger's Promise*, Safar al-Hawali denounced the arrival of foreign forces as an existential threat to Islam and Muslims. 'The Crusader invasion of the Arabian peninsula has already undermined the honour … of every Muslim,' he declared. 'It will not be long before your blood is shed with impunity or you declare your abandonment of your belief in God.'[13]

The war and the presence of foreign forces emboldened both Islamists and Western-educated liberals to speak out in favour of change. The liberals petitioned the king seeking political reform, women's rights and restrictions on the powers of the religious police. Not to be outdone, an alliance of Sahwa scholars and religious conservatives issued rival petitions attacking corruption and the un-Islamic character of Saudi foreign policy and calling for freedom of expression. It was clear which group the government feared more. Even after King Fahd issued a package of political reforms in 1992—introducing a quasi–constitutional document known as the Basic Law and setting up an unelected *majlis al-shura* (consultative council)—the pressure from the Islamists continued. In 1994 Al-Hawali and Al-Awda were arrested and, in response, hundreds of their followers took to the streets of Al-Awda's home town of Buraida, in a conservative region north of Riyadh, in what became known, with a touch of exaggeration, as the

Buraida *intifada* (uprising). In the eyes of its followers, this was the Sahwa's finest hour. The two leaders were held in jail for almost five years.[14]

When I visited the kingdom in 1994 the impact of these events was still palpable. Optimists could point to the fact that Kuwait had been freed. A great Western-led international army had saved the skins of the Gulf monarchs. (Wags claimed Saudi Arabia had a new national anthem, 'Onward, Christian Soldiers'.) Even then, four years on, King Fahd still felt the need to justify that fateful decision. 'The Lord of glory and grandeur helped us with soldiers from all parts of the world,' he told his newly-created *majlis al-shura*. 'Many said that the presence of foreign forces was wrong. But I say ... it was [a case of] extreme necessity.'[15]

The king was in his seventies, frail, diabetic and only intermittently in charge. The country was virtually bankrupt. It had contributed some $65 billion to the war effort (prompting the *Economist* to comment acidly that this was the age of 'rent-a-superpower'). And still its ally, the US, was pressing it to buy expensive weapons to show its gratitude.[16] What's more, the tremors of internal dissent were still being felt. The House of Saud was not out of the woods.

The Islamist opposition had a core of shared grievances, but it was hardly united. One part, the Sahwa, remained loyal to Al-Hawali and Al-Awda but after their imprisonment was thrown onto the defensive. Another part decamped to London. This was the Committee for the Defence of Legitimate Rights, set up inside the kingdom in 1993 by a group of six Islamists who advocated human rights (as defined by the Shari'a), the strengthening of religious institutions and the release of their brethren in jail. When the authorities clamped down on the CDLR most of its members were arrested, except for two who fled to London. These were Muhammad al-Masari and Saad al-Faqih (who a decade later was to call for the demonstration

I witnessed in Riyadh). In London, Masari—a big, bearded, ebullient former professor of physics—held court in a pizza house and kept in touch with like-minded people in Saudi Arabia by sending a stream of angry faxes denouncing princely corruption and maladministration.

A third element of the opposition was Bin Laden, who had grown increasingly disenchanted with the Al-Saud. After Iraqi forces had invaded Kuwait, he had offered to mobilise an army of *mujahidin* to chase them out. When the senior princes declined his offer and instead put their faith in America, he saw this as proof of their disloyalty to Islam and their unfitness to rule. He went into exile, first in Sudan, where he worked for Hasan al-Turabi, building roads and investing in Sudanese businesses, in return for which he was allowed to establish a headquarters and training camps. Then four years later, when under pressure from the US the Sudanese régime expelled him, he returned to where it had all begun, Afghanistan.

* * *

The Filipino taxi driver was wide-eyed. 'You know Al-Qatif, mister?'

I assured him, untruthfully, that I did—and off we went, from the modernity of Dhahran, a hub of the Saudi oil industry on the country's north-eastern coast, to the down-at-heels oasis town of Al-Qatif, most of whose citizens belong to the kingdom's Shi'ite minority. I arrived at an awkward time, as the faithful were being summoned to prayer, and dived into a small shop to wait for the moment to pass. (In Saudi Arabia Muslims are not only expected to pray five times a day. At prayer times the *mutawa*, or religious police, keep people off the streets and make sure shops are closed.) With some composure the young shopkeeper gave me a glance, looked at his watch and pulled down the shutters. As we sat in the half-darkness, I explained as delicately as possible who I was and why I was in town.

The Shi'a, who comprise ten to fifteen per cent of the Saudi population and are concentrated in the oil-rich Eastern Province, have long been treated as second-class citizens. Conservative Wahhabi scholars regard them as infidels: in the early days of the state, they advised King Abdel-Aziz to convert them to the true faith or deport them across the border. He declined to do either. But after the Khomeini revolution of 1979, the Shi'a were seen as a fifth column. There were violent demonstrations in Al-Qatif and other mainly Shi'a towns in late 1979 and early 1980. Some young Shi'a were electrified by the Iranian example, and the state clamped down on them hard.[17]

But by the early 1990s the situation had changed. King Fahd was far more worried about the new Sunni militancy than about any perceived Shi'a threat; the Shi'a themselves had begun to doubt whether radical Islamism offered them a better future; and Iran appeared to be no longer in the business of exporting its revolution. A more pragmatic movement emerged among the Saudi Shi'a, known as Al-Islah (Reform), which campaigned for human rights and constitutionalism rather than the overthrow of the Al-Saud. Shrewdly, Fahd struck a deal with Al-Islah in 1993, releasing some of its members from jail and promising to improve conditions in the Eastern Province. In return, the group's leaders ended their opposition activities, shut down their publications in London and Washington, and pledged to promote their community's rights through non-confrontational means.[18]

The people I met in Al-Qatif knew all about the deal, and grumbled that the Al-Saud had not kept their side of the bargain. The Shi'a were still restricted in their ability to build mosques and the communal meeting-places known as *husseiniyyas*. Wahhabi clerics and state-produced schoolbooks still referred to them in disparaging terms. Local services in Shi'a areas were poor, and unemployment high. (In the past the American oil company Aramco—which the Saudi state nationalised in 1988—had employed large numbers of local Shi'a, but it stopped doing so when the government came to see them as a potential threat.)

In June 1996 a truck bomb struck Khobar Towers, a US airforce housing compound in Dhahran, killing nineteen Americans. Suspicion at first fell on Al-Qaeda, but then shifted to a shadowy Shi'ite group called Saudi Hizbullah. Saudi and American officials eventually concluded, in the words of Bruce Riedel, a senior US official at the time, that 'Tehran ordered [the attack], Lebanon's Hizbullah provided the bomb-maker, and Saudi Hizbullah the terrorists'. Bin Laden later applauded the operation, but it seems unlikely that Al-Qaeda carried it out.[19]

The lesson of the attack appeared to be that, although most Saudi Shi'a had abandoned militant Islamism, a few remained bitter, vengeful and connected to radical networks elsewhere in the region.

＊

It was dusk at the Al-Hamra residential compound, a short taxi ride from downtown Riyadh. A soldier stood guard beside the entrance, and the compound walls had been enveloped in an extra ring of concrete slabs, to ward off attack. A few months earlier, on 12 May 2003, militants of Al-Qaeda in the Arabian Peninsula had carried out suicide car bombings of Al-Hamra and two other compounds in Riyadh, killing thirty-five people and wounding some 200. It was the start of a campaign of attacks against the régime and its security forces, and against the presence of Westerners in the kingdom, which was to cost some 300 lives over the next three or four years. The campaign amounted to 'the most serious and sustained domestic violence since the creation of modern Saudi Arabia in the early twentieth century'.[20]

Bin Laden had come a long way. From his exile in Afghanistan, where he allied himself with the Taliban régime, he had broken with the Al-Saud, and they with him. His anti–Soviet *jihad* had become an anti–Saudi *jihad* and then escalated into an anti–American *jihad*—an all-out, global struggle against what he termed the Crusader-Jewish alliance. In 1998 Bin Laden and his allies issued a declaration of war, urging Muslims to kill Americans, whether military or civilian, wherever they might be found. A few months later, Al-Qaeda carried out its first major operation, the truck-bomb suicide attacks against US embassies in Kenya and Tanzania which killed 220 people. The Clinton administration's response, launching missile strikes at a cluster of training camps in Afghanistan in the hope of killing Bin Laden, only helped turn him into an international icon of the Muslim revolt.

Al-Qaeda's operations in East Africa and Yemen—where a speedboat detonated a bomb against the hull of an American warship, the USS *Cole*, killing nineteen sailors—were the opening shots in its war against America, precursors of the attacks of 11 September 2001 against the superpower itself. The 9/11 attacks struck at symbols of American economic and military power (the Twin Towers and the Pentagon), at the same time killing close to 3,000 people and inflicting economic damage worth over $100 billion. Al-Qaeda's implicit message was that the United States—like the Soviet Union before it—was not invincible, and that the new *jihad* would hasten its collapse. Using Saudis, who comprised fifteen of the nineteen hijackers, struck a calculated blow at the US-Saudi alliance. In Congress, in the Washington think-tanks and in the media, Americans asked whether their long-time ally had not played a significant and sinister role in promoting radical Islamism.

For a full eighteen months after 9/11, the House of Saud was in denial. Saudi officials, journalists and academics countered the stream of accusations coming from the United States by protesting that they were being framed by America's Zionist-dominated media and political class. But after the attacks on their own soil, denial was no longer possible. The threat was not only real, it came from within.[21]

It is tempting to see the Saudi insurgency as Al-Qaeda's response to the American-led war in Iraq, which, despite serious misgivings, the kingdom had tacitly assisted. But a detailed study of the insurgency suggests that the Al-Qaeda leadership decided in early 2002—more than a year before the invasion of Iraq—to order Saudi militants in Afghanistan to return home and start preparing for a campaign of violence. The CIA apparently intercepted messages to this effect and warned the Saudis of the impending storm. The leading Al-Qaeda figure in the kingdom, the veteran jihadist Yusuf al-Uyayri, argued that he needed more time to prepare but was overruled by a leadership impatient for action.[22]

The Riyadh bombings were Saudi Arabia's 9/11, and they plunged the kingdom into a period of prolonged and painful soul-searching. Nothing in its history had prepared it for this. It had survived coup attempts in King Faisal's time by air-force officers inspired by the Nasserist dream of Arab unity. It had survived the ideological threat of Khomeini's Islamic revolution. It had survived the Iraqi invasion of Kuwait and the Saudi unrest this had unleashed, when the régime's Islamist opponents had used protests, petitions and tapes, but had not for the most part resorted to force. This time was different. The pillars of the House of Saud were being shaken.

With me as I sat watching the Al-Hamra compound was a Saudi taxi driver. This was a first; I had encountered plenty of Pakistani and Filipino drivers, but never a Saudi one. The man—let me call him Abdel-Aziz—had a big extended family to support and was moonlighting as a cab driver while holding down a daytime job in a government office. He had picked me up near the Kingdom Tower, where a few hours earlier the demonstration had taken place. As we drove past the smart shops at the foot of the tower, he scoffed, 'You visitors, you ought to see how real Saudis live.' And he proceeded to take me to the downbeat suburbs where poorer Saudis—many, like him, with large families—live side by side with the Asian migrant workers who work in shops and hotels, wait at tables and clean the streets. The drab apartment blocks and rubbish-strewn streets were a world away from the glitz of downtown Riyadh.

On our way back we passed a big fenced-off compound owned by one of the more prominent princes—the Ali Babas, as Abdel-Aziz called them—and he began to reel off their names. Only Crown Prince Abdullah, the country's *de facto* ruler during Fahd's extended illness, was exempt from the charge: he had a good heart, said Abdel-Aziz, even if he was surrounded by Ali Babas. We returned to the centre of Riyadh, its night-time skyline dominated by those two illuminated monoliths built by rival princes. 'The Twin Towers of Riyadh,' said Abdel-Aziz with a harsh laugh as he dropped me off beside Harvey Nichols.

* * *

Salafism, the Islam of the pious ancestors, had developed three distinct strains. There was its traditional core—conservative, introverted, apolitical—whose concern was with personal piety and whose leadership the House of Saud had effectively co-opted. There was the politicised but non-violent trend—the Sahwa—with its blend of Wahhabi creed and Muslim Brother-hood politics, which retained a following, especially among the young. And there was the newest, smallest and most dangerous strain, a militant *jihadi* Salafism which represented a threat not only to the United States and the West but to the Saudi monarchy itself. Salafism, whether in its violent or non-violent forms, appealed to the disaffected young because it offered them 'seemingly irrefutable religious certainty' and a Muslim identity 'infused with claims to authenticity'.[23]

In the aftermath of the Al-Hamra bombings, the House of Saud did battle with the Arabian wing of Al-Qaeda. In November 2003 there was another attack on a residential compound in Riyadh, killing eighteen people. In the months that followed, gunmen in a suburb of the capital seriously wounded my BBC colleague Frank Gardner and killed his cameraman. In June 2004 militants captured and subsequently beheaded an employee of the American defence contractor Lockheed Martin. Westerners—American, British, Irish, French, Italian— were deliberately singled out. Other attacks targeted the US consulate in Jeddah and buildings associated with the Saudi security forces. In 2006 the authorities foiled an attack on the kingdom's giant oil-processing facility at Abqaiq near the eastern coast: the first time Al-Qaeda had directly targeted the country's oil infrastructure.

By the following year, however, the Al-Saud, with the help of their American ally, appeared to have gained the upper hand. While arrests continued, the militants were finding it difficult to pull off successful operations. The authorities used 'hard power' to dismantle Al-Qaeda cells and kill or arrest its members and 'soft power' in an effort to re-educate and rehabilitate repentant jihadists.[24] But eradicating the Al-Qaeda ideology and winning the 'war of ideas' has proved to be a more difficult challenge. Moreover officials worry that Saudi militants returning from the conflict in neighbouring Iraq will rekindle the home-grown insurgency.

At the same time the Saudi authorities have struggled to deflect the charge made by their Western critics that they are more responsible for the rise of global jihadism than they care to admit. One persistent and much-debated item on the charge sheet is that the Wahhabi–dominated Saudi education system has indoctrinated young Saudis with hatred and suspicion of Christians, Jews and non-Wahhabi Muslims. In 2007 I visited Dr Hassan al-Maliki, a Saudi scholar who has devoted himself to the study of Wahhabism and its influence on Saudi school-books. He showed me examples of the Wahhabi obsession with *shirk* (idolatry): texts for teenagers warning against the untrustworthiness of the idolater, against marriage to an idolater or even doing business with one. (Strict Wahhabis consider Sufis and Shi'a idolaters, as well as Christians and Jews.) 'They are teaching the students,' he told me, 'that whoever disagrees with Wahhabism is either an infidel or a deviant and should repent or be killed.' Since the country is home to Shi'a, Sufi and other non-Wahhabi minorities, this, he said, was an attack on half of Saudi society.

Officials insisted offensive references had been expunged, but Maliki was not impressed. 'If you have fifty grenades in your house, and you remove half of them,' he said with an ironic laugh, 'you still have enough to blow up the house.' His critique of Wahhabism has incensed conservatives, who have done their best to silence him. He has been taken to court, imprisoned and banned from writing in the press. He has had to publish his books outside the country. After talking to me he was accused on a conservative website of giving interviews to the 'enemy media'.[25]

A second charge is that Saudis have played a significant—many would say the leading—role in funding Islamist extremism. After 9/11, US officials prodded the Saudis to regulate or shut down particular charities and take action against named individuals, but to little effect. Only after the bombings began in their own capital did Saudi officials belatedly stir themselves. They banned charities from sending money abroad—a move which hit organisations like WAMY hard, in some cases forcing them to shut down foreign branches or freeze their operations. No less controversially, the authorities removed collection boxes from mosques and shopping malls. These measures provoked a backlash of complaint, since many ordinary Saudis—for whom charitable giving is an essential Muslim duty—were convinced the government was cravenly doing America's bidding.

Two case studies show how strong the suspicions are concerning Saudi behaviour—and how hard it is to get solid enough proof to secure convictions in a courtroom. In 2002 the authorities in the United States shut down a Saudi charity called the Benevolence Foundation whose headquarters were in a suburb of Chicago. 'It was a big hoop-la,' recalls Sam Roe, an investigative journalist who covered the story for the *Chicago Tribune*. 'The US Attorney General at the time, John Ashcroft, flew out to Chicago and held a press conference. It was trumpeted as one of the first major victories in the "war on terrorism".'[26]

But it was, at best, an ambiguous victory. The Benevolence Foundation had been set up in the city a decade earlier by a wealthy Saudi businessman, Adel Batterjee. When, back home, the Saudi authorities started taking a closer look at his charitable activities, Batterjee handed over the running of the foundation to his right-hand man, a Syrian of Albanian extraction, Enaam Arnaout. The two men had met in Afghanistan in the 1980s when both had been helping Muslims fight the Soviet occupation.

The charity began to arouse the suspicions of the US authorities in the 1990s. But it was only after 9/11 that the case acquired any real urgency and attracted the attention of a star US attorney, Patrick Fitzgerald. Speaking to me at his office in a federal building in Chicago, Fitzgerald told me how he became convinced the Benevolence Foundation was an Al-Qaeda front. Documents found at its office in Bosnia, he said, described Al-Qaeda's founding meeting, its membership and the shipment of weapons.

But however strong the attorney's suspicions, he couldn't make the terrorism charges stick. In February 2003, on the eve of the trial, he struck a plea-bargain deal with Arnaout, who was convicted on a racketeering charge. He was found guilty of supplying boots and uniforms to Bosnian Muslim fighters, while claiming he was only helping civilians. It was a frustrating experience for the US authorities. They had shut down a charity about which they had the gravest suspicions, but had failed to prove its links to Al-Qaeda. While Arnaout served out his ten-year jail term, his former boss Adel Batterjee remained in the Saudi city of Jeddah, a wealthy and respected businessman. (There is even a street named after him.) On a visit to the city I phoned him but, like others before me, found he was unwilling to be interviewed.

***

In a second high-profile case, in 2004, the Riyadh headquarters of a major charity was closed, its director sacked and ten of its offices—stretching from the Netherlands to Indonesia—shut down. This was the Al-Haramain Foundation, a large and prestigious organisation set up in the 1990s which had close ties to the Saudi government and ruling family and at its height some fifty branches worldwide. I went to see Suliman al-Buthi, a Saudi in his mid-forties who had run the charity's branch in Ashland, Oregon, until it was shut down by the US authorities. He received me, Saudi–style, in a tent in a small compound in a residential part of Riyadh. This is the kind of *majlis*, or reception room, where Saudi men sit and chat and drink coffee. My Saudi host had taken the precaution of bringing along two high-powered American lawyers.

Al-Buthi is a wanted man—a 'specially designated global terrorist'. If he left Saudi Arabia, he would be arrested and taken for trial in the United States. He shrugs off the charge with a laugh. 'I never met Osama bin Laden,' he told me. 'I have never flown to any of these hot places—Bosnia or Chechnya or Afghanistan or Pakistan.' Al-Buthi's story is that the Al-Haramain branch was engaged in *da'wa*—spreading the word about Islam, through pamphlets and Qur'ans, to the good folk of Ashland, Oregon—and had nothing to do with terrorism. It was outrageous that American officials had shut the branch down and frozen its funds. If an individual Al-Haramain employee in, say, Bosnia or the Horn of Africa had been involved in suspicious activities, that was no fault of Al-Haramain itself. And if the Americans really had evidence against such people, they should produce it. Tellingly, Al-Buthi remains a respectable member of the Riyadh establishment, with a senior job in the health ministry. No Saudi official has ever accused him of funding terrorism and he has never been brought to trial before a Saudi court.

In Washington, I heard a rather different story from a former senior FBI official, Dennis Lormel. After the 9/11 attacks, when the issue suddenly became urgent, he built up what he regarded as a strong case against Al-Haramain only to find that Saudi officials 'didn't want to know'. It took two years of sustained American pressure before the Saudis were willing to act—and, even then, only after the shock of the bombings in their own capital. Lormel and some of his former colleagues believe the Saudis did too little, too late, and even now are failing to staunch the flow of funds to extremists. For all their protestations, 'they are just spinning the wheels', one former senior US government official told me.[27]

An essential ambiguity remains. Has the Saudi role been direct or indirect, witting or unwitting? Who exactly has been involved—individuals, organisations or the state? And, in any case, is it possible to track money with any accuracy through channels which are often so opaque? In 2004 the 9/11 Commission, the bi–partisan body appointed by Congress to investigate the suicide attacks of 2001, made a carefully-balanced judgement about the Saudi role: '[We] have found no evidence that the Saudi government as an institution or senior Saudi officials individually funded the organisation [Al-Qaeda] ... Still, Al-Qaeda found fertile fundraising ground in Saudi Arabia, where extreme religious views are common and charitable giving was both essential to the culture and subject to very limited oversight.'[28]

The root of the problem was that, over time, the pan-Islamic policies initiated by King Faisal in the 1960s had acquired a dynamic of their own. For decades, pan-Islamic solidarity, including generous charitable giving, was seen as impeccably virtuous—a matter on which the state, its citizens and the religious establishment were in accord. Indeed, before 9/11, the kingdom's American ally had turned a blind eye to Saudi support for Islamic militants, provided they were active against a common enemy (the Soviet Union, Saddam's Iraq, Khomeini's Iran). Only after 9/11 did such activities become reprehensible, or at least open to a different interpretation, by which time the waters had been thoroughly muddied. Where did good Islamic causes end and violent extremism begin? Who was to draw the distinction between extremism and legitimate resistance?

The Saudi princes have a case to answer. While the charges of some of their wilder critics are far-fetched, the fact remains that a flow of Saudi petrodollars has—with or without their knowledge—helped fund, legitimise and mobilise a movement of global *jihad*. Even if they were not directly responsible for the rise of Al-Qaeda, they cultivated the soil from which it sprang.

6

THE TURKISH EXCEPTION

At the scene of the crime, workmen are rebuilding the roof of the British consulate. But otherwise there is a deceptive normality. The shops are busy, the cafés and restaurants full. There is little sign of what happened on 20 November 2003, when a truck bomb went off in the historic Beyoğlu district of Istanbul, killing seventeen people, including the British consul, and leaving a three-metre-deep crater outside the consulate. The same day a second truck bomb struck a British-owned bank, HSBC. Five days earlier, the targets had been two synagogues in the city. In all, the four attacks killed sixty-three people, including the suicide bombers, and wounded more than 700.

The owner of a café beside the consulate tells me what happened. It was 11 a.m. and the city was still in shock after the first wave of bombings. He was standing at the entrance to the café when someone called him in to see why the television wasn't working. This probably saved his life. Moments later a pick-up truck packed with explosives rammed into the gates of the consulate. Those caught directly in the blast, including some of his customers, were killed, many others were wounded and the windows of neighbouring shops and bars were smashed.

Out of the blue, the global *jihad* had struck the Turkish republic.

Within hours of the first attacks, a Turkish journalist asked me in anger and bewilderment how it was possible his country had been targeted in this way. 'We even have an Islamist government,' he exclaimed, referring to Recep Tayyip Erdoğan's Justice and Development Party, which had swept to power the previous year. My reply, which can scarcely have consoled him, was that the bombers had not struck the Turkey of Erdoğan but the Turkey of Atatürk.[1]

***

Mustafa Kemal Atatürk created the Turkish exception. He turned a large Muslim country, which had played a not insignificant role in the story of Islam, into a secular republic modelled on European lines. In their responses to Western-style modernity, Atatürk and Khomeini stood at opposite poles, the one seeing it as the only future worth having, the other as, quite literally, the road to damnation.

The modern Turkish republic emerged in 1923 from the rubble of a once-great empire. At its height the Ottoman empire had been a superpower, dominating much of the Middle East and parts of southern and eastern Europe. But when it took Germany's side in the First World War, its fate was sealed. Defeat and dismemberment followed, and but for Atatürk's role in leading and mobilising a movement of national resistance Turkey might not have existed (or at least not in its current form). This helps explain the reverence he still inspires among modern Turks—which to visitors is all too redolent of a personality cult—and the embattled character of Turkish nationalism. If Turks are rather too prone to believe that the world (including the Western world) is against them, this is because, at the most crucial moment in their destiny, it was.

Mustafa Kemal was born in 1881, the son of a government clerk, in Salonika, in what is now Greece. At the age of fourteen he entered the military academy, graduating in 1905 and quickly rose through the ranks. He saw active service in Syria and the Balkans, witnessing for himself the growing resistance to Ottoman rule. Visits to France, Germany and Austria led him to contrast Europe and its achievements with a decrepit Ottoman empire sinking further and further into decline. What thrust him into the limelight was his role in the battle of Gallipoli during the First World War, when Turkish forces under his command held their own against the combined assault of troops from Britain, Australia and New Zealand. The eight-month battle exacted a terrible toll in lives, but it enabled Mustafa Kemal to emerge from the war as one of his country's few national heroes. He brought the same iron will to the struggle for independence.

The Atatürk story lends itself to hagiography. For a lively and less uncritical view one can turn to the fascinating eye-witness account of Halide Edib, who in later life became a distinguished writer, academician and social reformer. In the 1920s, during the struggle for independence, Edib worked as Atatürk's secretary and translator and was the only woman in his inner circle. She too was infected by what she called the 'magnificent madness' of nationalism, and she was in no doubt about Atatürk's ability to revive a dispirited nation. But if she admired the leader, she was frequently exasperated by the man. 'He was by turns cynical, suspicious, unscrupulous and satanically shrewd,' she wrote in her memoir, *The Turkish Ordeal*. 'He bullied. He indulged in cheap street-corner heroics. Possessing considerable though quite undistinguished histrionic ability, one moment he could pass as the perfect demagogue—a second George Washington—and the next moment fall into some Napoleonic attitude.'

'What an astounding man!' she reflected, after a meeting when he had talked everyone else in the room to exhaustion.

'Is he just some elemental force in a catastrophic form? Is there anything human about him at all? And how can this cyclone come to rest when the nation has reached its goal?'[2]

It was a prescient question. The cyclone did not come to rest. Instead, once the war had been won and the new republic established, Atatürk spent the remaining decade and a half of his life engaged in a one-man revolution to transform his country. His reforms were sweeping. He replaced Ottoman Turkish and its Arabic script with a modern form of the language, written in Latin letters, which he sought to purge of its Arabic and Persian accretions. He created Ankara as the new capital to replace Istanbul, which he considered decadent. He urged women to abandon the veil, and men the fez. He outlawed polygamy and gave women—in fact, imposed on them—the right to vote and hold public office. He introduced a radically new constitution, based on European models.

Central to his world-view was the rejection of subservience to religion and the men of religion. 'Can a civilised nation tolerate a crowd of people who let themselves be led by the nose by sheikhs, dervishes and the like,' he asked rhetorically, 'and who entrust their faith and their lives to fortune-tellers, magicians, witch doctors and amulet-makers?'[3] In this spirit, he banned the *tariqat*, the Sufi mystical orders. He insisted that the Muslim call to prayer should be in Turkish rather than Arabic. He abolished the Caliphate, the pan-Islamic institution which nominally at least had governed Muslim affairs for centuries, and declared Turkey to be a modern, secular, democratic republic. Few other Muslim societies, before or since, have undergone so radical a programme of modernisation and secularisation, pushed through by the dynamism and ruthlessness of a single-minded soldier-statesman.

* * *

When you enter Dolmabahçe Palace, whose elegant white façade stands beside the Bosphorus in Istanbul, it is as if time stood still. The clocks have stopped at 9.05 a.m.—the precise moment of Atatürk's death on 10 November 1938. This was his residence in Istanbul, the place where he stayed during his final illness and where he died at the age of fifty-eight, worn out by his tireless nation-building and a punishing lifestyle of drinking, partying and womanising.

But if Dolmabahçe played a role in the story of the founder of the modern Turkish republic, its earlier life has a very different significance. It was constructed in the middle of the nineteenth century because the sultans wanted to move from their old palace of Topkapı to one built in a new style—which meant a European style. They commissioned a well-known Armenian architect to build it and assigned the interior decoration to a Frenchman who went on to design the Paris Opera. The palace has 285 rooms, forty-three halls, six terraces and six *hammams* (Turkish baths). Its modernity is an apt symbol of the profound changes associated with the Tanzimat—the series of reforms carried out between the 1840s and the 1870s by Sultan Mahmud II and his successor Abdul-Majid which laid the foundations for Atatürk's programme of modernisation half a century later.

As in Egypt under Muhammad Ali, the place where modernisation began was the army. Sultan Mahmud, sometimes known as the Peter the Great of the Ottoman empire, created a new-style army under a Prussian adviser and sent cadets to study in Vienna and Paris. He reformed education, encouraging the learning of European languages, especially French. He sought to centralise government and reassert control over rebellious provinces. After Mahmud's death in 1839, Abdul-Majid accelerated the pace of educational reform and introduced a new legal code which put forward the revolutionary concept

125

of equality under the law, regardless of religion. In 1856 Abdul-Majid took up residence in the newly-built Dolmabahçe Palace, his own Versailles.

The Tanzimat met with resistance. The reforms were, after all, 'basically the forcible imposition, on a Muslim country, of practices and procedures derived from Europe, with the encouragement, if not the insistence, of European powers, and with the help of European experts and advisers'.[4] In daily life, they created a sometimes confusing world of two cultures. 'Culturally speaking,' the Turkish historian Halil Berktay told me, 'there was the opposition of *alla franca* [European-style] and *alla turca* [Turkish-style]. There was *alla franca* education, *alla turca* education—*alla franca* dress, *alla turca* dress. Toilets were *alla turca* or *alla franca*. Household lifestyles, whether you had a harem or not, this was a matter of *alla turca, alla franca*. So, in the late nineteenth and early twentieth centuries, the Tanzimat—the Turkish *perestroika*, as it were—created an enormous accumulation of modernisation, but at the same time created profound cultural cleavages.'[5]

The Ottoman reformers were pioneers. But if one of the prime purposes of their reforms was to hold the empire together, they failed. Arabs, Greeks and other subject peoples were determined to shake off the Turkish yoke. In a bid to stop the rot, a group of army officers overthrew Sultan Abdul-Hamid in what became known as the Young Turk Revolution of 1908–09. One of the supporters of the coup was Mustafa Kemal, then in his late twenties. The Young Turks, imbued with European notions of constitutional government, wanted to push the reform process much further. But it was too late to prevent the empire's collapse—and defeat in the First World War administered the *coup de grâce*.

Historians like to remind us that Atatürk was the inheritor and beneficiary of these earlier efforts at reform. But his purpose was very different. Unlike his predecessors, he rejected the empire and all it stood for—corruption, decline, backwardness, which were linked in his mind to the reactionary power of religion—in favour of modern nationalism and the European-style nation-state. Turks could no longer rule a baggy multi–ethnic, multi–cultural empire loosely held together by Islam and Islamic law; but they *could* become masters of their destiny in a new nation-state, shorn of empire and (largely) of troublesome minorities, and whole-heartedly committed to Western-style modernisation. His aim was nothing less than to pluck Turkey from the Muslim East and make it part of the modern West: it was, in Bernard Lewis's words, 'a large-scale, deliberate attempt to take a whole nation across the frontier from one civilisation to another'.[6] What is remarkable is not that, after Atatürk's death, crucial elements of his legacy came under challenge—which was surely inevitable—but that so much has endured.

* * *

Zeliha is a feisty seventeen-year-old. Sitting at home with her family in their neat and modest apartment, she tells me why she will not go to school unless she can wear a headscarf. 'When the new term started,' she says, 'I went to school in the normal way. But there were riot police—RoboCops—in front of the school. They told us we could only go in if we took off our headscarves.'

But shouldn't she, I ask, obey the state, which has been secular since Atatürk's time? 'I don't feel I have to comply with what the state says,' Zeliha replies defiantly. 'This is my faith—and I want to live by it. Turkey has to be a free country. There shouldn't be any discrimination on the grounds of language, religion or race.'[7]

Only in France has the headscarf been as fiercely contested as in Turkey. For staunch Kemalists—followers of Mustafa

127

Kemal's nationalist tradition—it is a deliberate affront to the secular values of the Turkish republic. But Zeliha claims she is entitled to cover her head as a basic human right. It is her personal choice, she insists; no group or party has put her up to it. 'If I have to choose between my career and my headscarf,' she tells me, 'I'll choose my headscarf.'

It is hard to know if she is indeed acting alone. But certainly she must draw some encouragement from the significant changes which have been under way in Turkey since Atatürk's death in 1938. Although his modernising reforms were far-reaching, their impact was uneven. He left behind a nation of twelve million, eighty per cent of whom were illiterate.[8] As one Turkish scholar puts it, 'Kemalist secularism barely infiltrated Turkish society at large. The rural and pious masses of Anatolia remained largely unaffected by the cultural re-engineering taking place in Ankara; it was the military, the government bureaucracy, and the urban bourgeoisie who adapted most readily to Kemalism's thorough westernisation.

'Winning hearts and minds in the countryside,' he goes on, 'would have required the use of traditional and religious symbols, but those were anathema to the Turkish republic's founding fathers. In short order, the cultural gap between the Kemalist center and the Anatolian periphery had become insurmountable.'[9]

Islam—or, more precisely, organised Islam—gradually made a comeback. One factor was that the Sufi orders, the *tariqat*, still retained a strong following, especially in rural areas, despite Atatürk's efforts to ban them. Another was that, with the introduction of multi–party politics in the 1950s, politicians began to compete for Muslim votes, especially in the more conservative towns and villages of Anatolia. And a third, more surprising factor is that the Turkish military—which has traditionally seen itself as the ultimate guardian of Kemalism—

unwittingly played into the hands of the Islamists. The generals seized power in 1980—their third intervention in as many decades—in order to end the violence between left and right which had brought the country to the brink of civil war. In the aftermath of the coup they set out to foster a moderate, nationalist Islam as a counterweight to communist and other left-wing tendencies, to Kurdish nationalism in the south-east of the country—and to the new revolutionary Islam emanating from Iran. Thus was born what came to be known as the 'Turkish-Islamic synthesis': a form of 'depoliticised Turkish-Islamic culture' that the generals hoped would 'provide the basis for a unified, strong and stable state'.[10]

The 1980s were a period of significant political, economic and social change. Under Turgut Özal, the country enjoyed sustained export-driven growth and built close political and economic ties to Saudi Arabia and the other big oil producers of the Gulf. At the same time, Turkey's Islamic revival gathered pace. Özal's policies encouraged the emergence of a new middle class, more pious than the traditional élite and eager to claim its share of economic and political power. Meanwhile massive migration from rural Anatolia created large makeshift settlements, known as *gecekondu*, on the edges of the big cities. Many migrants brought with them the conservative religious values of their towns and villages.

The beneficiary of this social transformation was an Islamic movement which, in 1983, acquired a new leadership with the birth of Refah—the Welfare Party. Refah could rely not only on the piety of the new middle class but on voters' growing disenchantment with the traditional parties of centre-right and centre-left, which they saw as corrupt and self-serving. As Refah built up grass-roots support, it came to pose a serious challenge to these parties' traditional monopoly of power. In 1996, to the consternation of the secular establishment, Refah's avuncular, white-haired, seventy-year-old leader, Necmettin Erbakan, became Turkey's first Islamist prime minister. Erbakan's brand of populist, anti–Western Islam was not at all what the generals had had in mind. With his vague but appealing slogan of *adil düzen*—the just order—he scarcely concealed his nostalgia for the Ottoman past, his disdain for the Kemalist order and his conviction that Islamic civilisation was superior to anything the West might have to offer.

Whether he really had a sinister Islamist agenda to subvert the secular state or simply overplayed his hand is debatable. He certainly antagonised secularists with his populist gestures and extravagant Islamist rhetoric. He favoured the headscarf, wanted to end interest rates and called for a *jihad* to liberate Jerusalem. He criticised the European Union and NATO, advocating instead an Islamic common market and an Islamic NATO. He sought closer ties with Iran, Libya and Saddam Hussein's Iraq. Eventually, after only a year in office, pressure from the military forced him to resign. Refah was subsequently banned.[11]

The result was that the Islamic movement split. A conservative rump remained loyal to Erbakan, while a more moderate wing emerged under Recep Tayyip Erdoğan and his colleague Abdullah Gül, who eventually formed the Justice and Development Party in 2001. Erdoğan and Gül learned two important lessons from Erbakan's demise: that Turkish Muslims had to make a historic compromise with the secular state, and that Turkey's destiny lay in the European Union.

Ali Bulaç, an innovative Muslim intellectual and columnist with the Islamist newspaper *Zaman*, gave me his interpretation of the military's 'silent' coup of 1997. 'It showed once again that the bureaucracy is the ultimate arbiter. Just as in Ottoman times, it was the state which decided when and how things would change. The society and the individual had no say in the matter. The Turkish state—and this is the crucial point—has never changed except as a result of external pressure. Europe used to press the Ottoman empire to reform—it was forced to change, it didn't want to change. But now, for the first time, in the debate over whether to join the European Union, Europe and the Turkish society are calling for the same thing—and the bureaucracy is finding itself squeezed.'[12]

Turkish Islamists had initially derided the European Union as a 'Christian club'. But after the ousting of Erbakan they changed their minds, seeing it as an essential ally in the struggle for far-reaching reform. Their Kemalist critics saw their apparent change of heart as a trick designed to conceal their real aim—to subvert the secular state and impose Islamic law.

* * *

Kemalism is guarded by a coalition of powerful forces in the judiciary, the bureaucracy, the media and, above all, the military. This coalition is not monolithic—any more than the country's multi–faceted Islamic movement is—but within it the Turkish generals are without doubt the most important element. Whenever they have felt the republic was in danger, they have intervened to oust civilian governments. During the Cold War they did so three times, in the coups of 1960, 1971 and 1980. But even when civilians have been nominally in charge, the military has remained a significant presence in the wings and has not hesitated to make known its views on public affairs.

I visit Istanbul's Harb Akademisi—the War College—to meet a retired general, Sabri Yirmibeşoğlu. At the entrance, security is tight. A smartly-dressed young soldier gets into the car to accompany us as we go through the gates. Once inside, you feel you have entered an up-market housing complex, with pleasant trees and neat undulating lawns. The military like to live in some style, with their own apartment blocks and subsidised shops—all enclosed within a carefully-guarded compound.

General Sabri is a short, stocky man in his seventies. He greets me and takes me to the officers' club where we sit and talk. He is a loyal disciple of Atatürk, but anxious to make Kemalism seem palatable to the new generation. 'I keep telling the young people today that if they take Kemalism as a dogma, they might find it boring. Atatürk's ideas can be adapted to meet the needs of the modern world.' But when it comes to Zeliha and her headscarf, he is unyielding. 'They're using the headscarf as a provocation. They're politicising the whole thing—and the Turkish people are not comfortable with that. In Turkey it's not forbidden to cover your hair or your body. But the Turkish public gets upset when this is done in the public sphere—and in public education—and when the headscarf is used as a political symbol.'

I come away realising that two worlds are in collision—an older world of nationalist certainties, in which the wise and powerful state knows best, and a newer, more questioning world in which religion and religious identity have become more assertive. In the clash between Zeliha and the general, neither is willing to compromise.[13]

* * *

One of the most important battlegrounds in the contest between Muslims and secularists is the classroom. A visit to two very different state-run secondary schools provides a window onto the Turkish *kulturkampf*. The first is a bright, modern school of some 2,000 students, both boys and girls, between the ages of fourteen and seventeen. Near the entrance is the familiar bust of Atatürk and below it his dictum 'Science is the true guide in life'. The school is well-equipped and the curriculum progressive. In the biology class I ask the teacher how she handles Darwin's theory of evolution—something many orthodox Muslims, like many orthodox Christians, do not accept. 'We stick to the curriculum,' she replies, 'and the curriculum tells us to teach it.'[14]

The second school is older and shabbier than the first. Near the entrance is the same bust of Atatürk, with the same slogan beneath it. But there the similarity ends. Turkey has two types of secondary school, the standard kind and those known as *imam-hatip* schools. These were originally designed to produce *imams* (prayer leaders) and *hatips* (preachers). But in fact the boys and girls who come here won't necessarily enter either of these professions. I ask the head teacher how his school differs from an ordinary secondary school. 'We follow the principles of Atatürk,' he replies. 'We teach the same curriculum as the other state schools. The only difference is that we add religious instruction.'

I ask if the school teaches Darwin's theory of evolution. 'Yes, of course,' he replies, 'even though I personally disagree with Darwin's theory. But in the Islamic philosophy class, the students hear what the Qur'an says—that God created the world—so they hear both views and they can make up their own minds.'

It is hard to believe that Atatürk would have approved. But then he would not have wanted *imam-hatip* schools in the first place. They were set up in the early 1950s, more than a decade after his death, because Turkish politicians, hungry for votes, saw there was demand for them. Conservative families wanted their children to have a religious element in their education, regardless of whether they went on to become *imams* or *hatips*.[15]

I ask the head teacher about the headscarf affair, which has meant that girls like Zeliha can't go to school at all. He says there's no problem at his school—they've been implementing the ban for several years. So why, I ask, is there a problem at other *imam-hatip* schools? He looks distinctly embarrassed. A woman-from-the-ministry has been sitting in on the interview, and he glances at her anxiously. He says it's an issue he'd rather not discuss.

* * *

Even as I was visiting the schools, a new force was taking shape in Turkish politics, a party which had emerged from the Islamist movement, radically rebranded itself and was now on the verge of winning power. This was the Justice and Development Party (AKP) of Recep Tayyip Erdoğan and Abdullah Gül. Erdoğan and Gül had worked with Erbakan and his Refah party in the 1990s, and undoubtedly shared some of his Islamist views. But they represented a younger and more pragmatic generation within Refah who realised they could never win over Turks outside their core constituency—or keep the military at bay—unless they jettisoned their Islamist baggage. Their strategy was to present themselves not as a religious movement but as a party of social conservatives committed unequivocally to democracy, the free market and Europe, which they had come to see 'as the primary anchor of Turkish democracy and modernisation'.[16]

It was a shrewd calculation, since there were now plenty of voters—above all, among the middle class—who were tired of the stale, self-seeking politics of left and right and ready to give the AKP a chance. In 2002 the party came to power with an impressive thirty-seven per cent of the votes. (Traditionally, Turkish elections had failed to produce a clear winner, instead spawning quarrelsome and unstable coalition governments.)

Erdoğan and his colleagues embarked on wide-ranging reforms designed to improve human rights, protect minorities, promote economic growth and strengthen civilian control of the military—all with an eye to increasing Turkey's chances of joining the European Union. EU membership was seen not just as a desirable goal but as a powerful catalyst for reform. As one AKP adviser admitted candidly, 'As a party, we wish to see a more democratic Turkey, but we have to face the fact that our internal dynamics are not sufficient enough to achieve this. The EU compensates for insufficient internal dynamism.'[17]

The party's policies won acclaim at home and abroad. The Bush administration, anxious in the aftermath of 9/11 to promote a positive model in the Muslim world, hailed Turkey's synthesis of Islam, democracy and capitalism. (This did not prevent serious tensions in US-Turkish relations, especially when the Turkish parliament refused to allow US forces to use southern Turkey as a springboard for attacking Iraq in 2003.) Many Turks who were by no means sympathetic to the AKP's Islamist past were impressed by its performance.

But, five years after its election victory, an extraordinary sequence of events showed that, for all the party's undoubted achievements, the old rifts between Islam and secularism and between civilian governments and the military had not been healed. The generals had always suspected that the party harboured a secret Islamist agenda, and they claimed to see proof of this when, in 2007, it nominated Abdullah Gül—who as foreign minister had led the drive to join the EU—for the post of president. The Turkish presidency is largely ceremonial but has traditionally been occupied by a secularist. Gül was a former Islamist whose wife wore a headscarf. Kemalists, both civilian and military, launched a concerted campaign to prevent him winning this symbolic prize.

On 27 April, after weeks of tension between the two camps, the military warned in a statement on their official website that, if necessary, 'they [would] not hesitate to make their position and stance abundantly clear as the absolute defenders of secularism'. But this 'e-coup'—as the Turkish media dubbed it—backfired. General elections were brought forward, the AKP increased its share of the vote to forty-seven per cent—

and Gül duly became president. It was, as one Turkish analyst put it, 'a victory for the new democratic, pro-market, and globally integrated Turkey over the old authoritarian, statist and introverted one'.[18]

But the crisis raised troubling questions about whether cohabitation is possible between the military and a post-Islamist party—and whether Turkey can indeed produce a successful synthesis of Islam, democracy and the market economy. At the same time, it coincided with growing Turkish disenchantment with the EU, whose member-states were badly divided over whether they should admit Turkey to membership, despite having formally acknowledged its eligibility. Polls had indicated in 2005 that three-quarters of Turks were enthusiastic about joining Europe. By 2007, the figure had slumped to forty per cent.

* * *

The workshop in Istanbul was disguised as a detergent factory. In fact it was making bombs. Here a secretive group of conspirators worked for eighteen months—mostly at night—planning the series of devastating truck-bomb attacks which struck the city in November 2003.[19]

As elsewhere in the Muslim world, Islamism in Turkey has moved along a number of different trajectories. The political Islam of the 1980s produced, as we have seen, Refah, the movement from which emerged the more pragmatic and reform-minded Justice and Development Party. But, at the same time, conflicts inside and outside Turkey helped spawn a much more radical form of Islamism, part of which eventually found common cause with Al-Qaeda.

At home, a radicalising factor was the long and dirty war waged in south-east Turkey between the Turkish security forces and the militant Kurdish group the PKK, or Kurdistan Workers' Party. The conflict began in 1984 and over the next two and a half decades claimed some 40,000 lives and displaced many more. In the late 1980s a rival to the PKK emerged in the form of Hizbullah (a Sunni Islamist group often referred to as Turkish Hizbullah, to distinguish it from the Lebanese Shi'ite movement of the same name). The authorities at first turned a blind eye to it; indeed some allege they used it as a counter-weight to the secular-leftist PKK. Later, when the tide seemed to turn in the war against the PKK after its leader Abdullah Öcalan was captured in 1999, the security forces cracked down on Hizbullah and claimed to have crushed it. Although weakened, however, it continues to draw support from Kurds in the south-east, where religion is becoming a stronger force.[20]

Meanwhile hundreds of Turks fought in Afghanistan, Bosnia, Chechnya and Iraq, receiving training and acquiring links with radical Islamist networks, including Al-Qaeda. Typical of the new breed was Habib Akdaş. Born in the mainly Kurdish town of Bingöl in eastern Turkey in 1973, Akdaş fought in Bosnia and Chechnya. In the late 1990s he went to Afghanistan, where he became the leader of a group of Turks at an Al-Qaeda training camp. Akdaş was to take charge of the group which carried out the Istanbul bombings.

The origins of the plot date back to September 2001, just a few days before the attacks of 9/11, when Akdaş and a group of other Turks had a breakfast meeting with Osama bin Laden in a single-storey mud-brick house in Kandahar, in southern Afghanistan. They sought and received his blessing for an operation against Western and Israeli targets in Turkey. While they revered the Al-Qaeda leader—and were eventually to receive $150,000 from Al-Qaeda to carry out the attacks—the preparation and execution of the plot were their own. Like other Al-Qaeda 'franchises' around the world, this was an essentially home-grown group which shared Bin Laden's ideology without formally belonging to his organisation. In any case, after the 9/11 attacks and the American invasion of Afghanistan, the Al-Qaeda leadership had other, more pressing issues on their mind.

Once he had returned home, Akdaş was joined by a former Turkish Hizbullah official, Azad Ekinci, and under their leadership the plot began to take shape. Most members of the group they brought together were Kurds in their late twenties or early thirties from eastern and south-eastern Turkey, the country's poorest and traditionally most conservative regions. Their link with Al-Qaeda was a Syrian called Louai Sakka—codenamed Alaaddin—who brought them $100,000 rolled up in a sock. Sakka was a Turkish speaker, a hardened *jihadi* who was reputed to be a master of disguise and who travelled frequently between Syria and Turkey.

It appears the cell toyed with the idea of attacking American targets such as the NATO airbase at İncirlik, on the southern coast, or the US consulate in Istanbul. But these were well guarded, so they chose softer targets—synagogues, a bank and the British consulate—symbols, in their eyes, of the hated 'Crusader-Jewish' alliance against Islam. (The initial plan had included an attack on Israeli passengers disembarking from a cruise ship in Alanya, a resort on Turkey's southern coast. But when the ship didn't show up because of bad weather, the idea was abandoned.) Meeting at their rented detergent factory in Istanbul, the group chose the four suicide bombers—three of whom had been to Pakistan where they reportedly became radical Salafis—mixed the explosives and loaded them onto pick-up trucks.

The attacks were devastating and threatened to open a new front in the global *jihad*. But they were also amateurish. Akdaş's recruits were scarcely an A-team. Although they did kill a few of their intended victims—six Jewish worshippers and three Britons, including the British consul—all the other casualties were Turkish Muslim passers-by. Moreover the Turkish authorities had a lucky break when they captured one of the group's look-out men, Yusuf Polat, as he tried to leave the country. In 2005 they caught a much bigger fish, Louai Sakka. Two other conspirators gave themselves up, apparently out of remorse over the loss of Muslim lives. Of the ringleaders, Azad Ekıncı evaded capture and Habib Akdaş went to Iraq, where he was reportedly killed in an American air strike while fighting in the town of Fallujah.

So the cell was quickly smashed, and there was little sign that it had enjoyed wider support within Turkish society. Since then, however, there have been further arrests of Al-Qaeda suspects and evidence of continuing links between Islamist militants at home and Turks fighting in Iraq. All in all, the lessons from the Istanbul bombings were sobering. It was bad enough that the jihadists were now able to recruit disaffected Turks and Kurds for their foreign wars. Worse still, the bombings suggested that Turkey itself—with its secular tradition, its membership of NATO and its ties to both the United States and Israel—was now in the firing-line.

* * *

The Turkish exception endures. No other part of the Muslim world—with the sole exception of the Muslim republics of the former Soviet Union—has been thrust so abruptly into secular modernity. No other has joined NATO and aspires to join the European Union. But even if Turkey is one of a kind, what happens there is of significance in the wider Muslim world. Given the reassertion of Islam in Turkey since the 1970s, the country's fortunes are being watched closely by Muslim intellectuals and activists elsewhere, as well as by Western policy-

7

MUSLIM ARCHIPELAGO

Colonel Sam was trying hard. As we approached the village, Thai flags fluttered at regular intervals by the roadside. A welcoming committee of villagers stood awkwardly waiting for the foreign visitors. Colonel Sam gave them a pep talk and they clapped dutifully.

This was the Potemkin village of southern Thailand.

Look at the map, and the scattered islands of south-east Asia are like fragments of a broken cup. The region has been called the Muslim archipelago. Stretching from southern Thailand down through the Malay peninsula and Singapore and across the great expanse of Indonesia to the southern Philippines, it is home to a largely Malay-speaking Muslim community comprising about one-fifth of the Islamic world.

Islam came late to the region, brought by merchants from the Indian sub-continent, China and Arabia in the twelfth and thirteenth centuries. It arrived in an area where Hinduism and Buddhism were already well established. It had to fit in, and over time it did, blending an often Sufi–tinged practice of the faith with elements of pre-existing religions and cultures. The region's dominant tradition is one of cultural coexistence and pluralism, even if its history has been scarred by acts of intolerance and violence.

* * *

'The people love the army,' said Colonel Sam with a wide grin. 'They *love* the army.' It was the autumn of 2004. The colonel, a tall, self-confident man, was a military spokesman in southern Thailand, where a few months earlier a Muslim insurgency had revived. By the 'people' Colonel Sam meant the local Muslims. Most Thais are Buddhist, but in the country's 'deep south'—the three southern provinces bordering Malaysia—the majority are both Muslim and ethnic Malay. Once a Muslim sultanate, the region was formally annexed by the Thai state in the early years of the twentieth century. Local grievances flared into a nationalist rebellion in the 1960s which lasted virtually two decades. Now some observers were wondering whether the latest insurgency—which between 2004 and 2009 was to claim more than 3,500 lives—might one day morph into a holy war.

The colonel saw things differently. Sitting in his car cradling a revolver in his lap, he insisted the violence was the work of criminals, smugglers and drug traffickers: the ordinary people loved the Thai army. Perhaps sensing my scepticism, he offered to take me on a guided tour. In the mixed villages of the south, Muslims and Buddhists had by and large coexisted peacefully for decades. Now shadowy Muslim militants were targeting Thai soldiers and civilians, including Buddhist monks, and Muslims deemed to be collaborators. Bombings and drive-by shootings and, more ominously, beheadings had driven a wedge between the two communities. The army was helping local people set up self-defence groups. The colonel took me to a firing range where villagers were being trained using old rifles. He assured me the militia was made up of both Muslims and Buddhists. When I asked where the Muslims were, he said it was prayer time and they were at the mosque.

We drove on to the Potemkin village: a military construct designed to impress CNN and the BBC. This time there were one or two Muslims among the awaiting villagers. They smiled for the cameras. A large bare-headed woman advanced towards me with a huge melon: a present to the visiting journalist and proof that the army had, as the colonel claimed, improved the agricultural life of the people. But the effect was unconvincing. The village was as artificial as a film-set.[1]

* * *

Who the militants are is a puzzle. Neither the Thai authorities nor independent experts appear to know with any certainty. The militants make no statements of responsibility for attacks and issue no demands. But even if there are several groups—some new, others with apparent links to older nationalist factions—there seems to be some degree of co-ordination. On a single day in April 2004, groups of Muslim men across the deep south launched simultaneous attacks on Thai army posts. More than a hundred of them were killed. Since they were armed with little more than knives, machetes and magic potions, these were virtually suicide missions.

A few months after the event, I visited the historic Kru-Ze mosque in the town of Pattani, where thirty-two of the militants had taken refuge. After a nine-hour stand-off, government troops threw grenades into the mosque and then stormed it, killing all those inside. Although the militants were not unarmed—they had a handful of stolen rifles and a grenade-launcher—local people were furious that the Thai army had desecrated a much-revered building. Most of those who died seem to have been naïve young men who had fallen under the influence of a local Muslim teacher, Ustadz Soh, who subsequently disappeared. Whether he was part of some wider organisation was not clear.[2]

One evening, in a village near Pattani, I walked through the jungle to the simple home of Nur, a mother of six whose husband Muhammad was among those who had died that day in April 2004. 'All he said was that he was going to a religious meeting,' she told me. 'He was a good man, very quiet and gentle and straightforward. Perhaps he was tricked—some people are saying that.' Even the families seemed none the wiser about why their men-folk had acted as they did.

The Muslims of the south feel the Thai state has failed to acknowledge their distinct culture and history. They also feel economically marginalised. They benefit little if at all from the tourist revenues enjoyed by the popular beach resorts further north. Though a minority profit from crime, corruption and cross-border smuggling, many local people are dependent on traditional forms of livelihood such as rubber-tapping and fishing.

I visited a small fishing village of a few thousand people—mostly Muslims, but with a few Buddhist families living in their midst. On a hot day, with a breeze coming in from the sea as the fishermen brought in their catch, it seemed idyllic. But I soon heard the villagers' complaints. They faced tough competition from 'outsiders'—Thai fishermen coming down from the north who were rapidly depleting stocks with their modern methods. As a result, people were looking for work outside the village. They were taking menial jobs in the towns or crossing the border to find work in Malaysia.

But if economic marginalisation is a contributory factor, the conflict is at root political, driven by a deep sense of injustice. And, by common consent, the heavy-handed response to the insurgency by the government of Thaksin Shinawatra, prime minister from 2001 until his overthrow in a military coup in 2006, had only made things worse. Thaksin, a former police-man, was a self-made millionaire who became a populist strongman. As I travelled through the south in 2004, I saw prominent pictures of him displayed at regular intervals by the roadside. His improbably named party, 'Thais Love Thais', clearly enjoyed little support among Muslims.

I visited the police station in the small border town of Tak Bai. Here a few weeks earlier, in October 2004, over 2,000 Muslim demonstrators had gathered to protest at the arrest of six local men from whom the police had seized a number of weapons. Eye-witnesses told me what had happened next. In an attempt to disperse the crowd, the police turned water cannon on them and then opened fire, killing seven of the protestors. Then they bundled more than a thousand others into army trucks, piling them on top of one another, sometimes four deep. By the time the trucks reached an army base further north, many had died of suffocation. The final death toll was eighty-five. The horror of Tak Bai, during the Muslim fasting month of Ramadan, brought southern Thailand briefly to the world's attention. In nearby villages one could sense the sullen resentment of the army's pervasive presence and of the Thaksin government, seen as wholly unsympathetic to Muslim grievances.[3]

Could this local conflict be exploited by the global jihadists and their regional allies? Globalisation has meant that the south, once a backwater, is now in touch with world events. 'When we see on TV what the Americans are doing to the Iraqis and what the Israelis are doing to the Palestinians,' a local Muslim academic told me, 'it reminds us of what the Thai soldiers are doing here.' Local grievances tap into global ones, and vice versa.

After Thaksin's overthrow, the country's new military rulers offered an olive branch to the southern Muslims. The general who led the coup visited the south and publicly apologised for the errors of the past. But despite the offer of a dialogue, the violence continued.

An authoritative recent account of the insurgency concludes that it has been disastrously mishandled by both the Thai army and the authorities in Bangkok. They have alienated the local population through the excesses of the security forces and through a crude and ultimately unsuccessful attempt to co-opt a local Muslim élite. As a result, the militants are now 'in the ascendant' and enjoy the passive support of a large part of the population. Much of the violence is localised, with little or no wider co-ordination. 'There [are] no real masterminds.' At root, the problem is neither a religious conflict nor part of a global *jihad*, but stems from the Thai state's lack of legitimacy in the south. The insurgency is unlikely to end without a resolution of this crisis of legitimacy.[4]

* * *

Across the border, in the Malaysian capital Kuala Lumpur, a packed meeting was under way organised by the city's lawyers. They had invited as their guest of honour the country's best-known opposition figure, Anwar Ibrahim.

Malaysia in 2004 was in transition. The forceful and some-times acerbic Mahathir Muhammad, who as prime minister from 1981 had pushed and pulled his compatriots into a 'Muslim modernity', had stepped aside and been succeeded by the more staid and cautious Abdullah Badawi. In a gesture of reconciliation, the authorities had released Anwar Ibrahim from prison. Anwar had been Mahathir's deputy and presumed heir, but after the two men fell out he was jailed in 1998 on corruption and sodomy charges which many saw as politically motivated. Now, it seemed, there was to be a time of healing.

Although pale and weak after his six years in solitary confinement, the fifty-seven-year-old Anwar could still hold an audience. The meeting was a chance for him to thank the lawyers for their support during his incarceration. But while celebrating his release as a belated victory for the rule of law, the lawyers were not inclined to give him an easy ride. They wanted to know if he was still an Islamist. In the past, as a charismatic Muslim leader, he had rallied huge crowds with his battle-cry of *reformasi* (reformation, or radical change). So where did he stand now? Was he for a secular state, which the country had largely been since independence, or an Islamic state, which many felt it was in the process of becoming? He ducked and weaved, trying to have it both ways.[5]

Malaysia's English-speaking liberal lawyers are children of the British Raj in south-east Asia. For the British, the attraction of the Malay peninsula was not the inhospitable jungle of the interior but the Malacca straits, the strategic waterway and artery of trade at its southern tip. They arrived on the scene in 1786, taking control of Penang, an island in the straits, for use as a naval base. Then, in 1819, they established a foothold on the island of Singapore. Not long afterwards, the British and the Dutch struck a deal: the latter would keep Java and Sumatra (the two most populous islands of what is now Indonesia) and the much-prized Spice Islands (the modern-day Moluccas), leaving the British in control of the Malay peninsula and Singapore, which in time became one of the world's great ports.

Gradually even the hinterland of the peninsula, with its dense jungle and Muslim population ruled by local sultans, came under British control. There were two important sources of wealth: tin and rubber. The rubber tree was brought over from Kew Gardens in 1877, and Malayan rubber was soon providing tyres for the world's rapidly-growing car industry. By bringing in Chinese and Indian workers to clear the jungle for the new rubber plantations, the British also changed the country's ethnic composition. Over time, the rural Malays came to feel threatened by the role of the Chinese in the economy.[6]

Japan's initial victories in the Second World War were traumatic for the region. In 1942 it inflicted a humiliating defeat on Britain by capturing Malaya and Singapore and holding them for three years. The Japanese regarded China as a detested regional enemy and treated the Chinese in Malaya with great brutality. After the war the British tried to re-order the country's affairs by proposing a new Malayan Union with equal citizenship for all, including the Chinese. The Muslim Malays reacted with alarm and, as a defence mechanism, created the United Malays National Organisation (UMNO), which fought successfully to have the Malayan Union proposal scrapped. UMNO's slogan and *raison d'être* was 'Malaya for the Malays'. Under the leadership of a shrewd aristocratic playboy, Tunku Abdul Rahman, it was the vehicle through which Malaya eventually gained independence from Britain in 1957. (In 1963 an enlarged federated state was created, incorporating parts of Borneo and initially Singapore, under the new name Malaysia. But Tunku Abdul Rahman soon came to see the shrewd Singaporean leader Lee Kuan Yew as a dangerous rival. Singapore was expelled from the federation and became an independent state.)

Kuala Lumpur is today a lively, thrusting city, dominated by its famous Petronas twin towers. To get a sense of the project that Mahathir pursued so single-mindedly in the 1980s and 1990s, I visited the International Islamic University Malaysia. The IIUM is an impressively modern, high-tech structure dating from 1983, which has some 20,000 students from ninety-six countries. The language of instruction is English. The rector, Kamal Hassan, told me the IIUM was the embodiment of Mahathir's vision of a successful Malaysian modernity imbued with the values of Islam. The university's mission statement sets out the bold aim of 'reforming the contemporary Muslim mentality and integrating Islamic Revealed Knowledge and Human Sciences in a positive manner'.

But behind the country's high-tech exterior and colourful multi–cultural diversity is an inescapable reality, in part a legacy

of colonial rule—the racial basis of its politics. The achievement of independence did not allay Malay mistrust of the
Chinese. In 1969 there were serious riots in Kuala Lumpur
which, according to official figures, left 177 people dead. In
response, the government introduced a set of policies which
favoured the *bumiputra*, or sons of the soil—the Muslim Malays
who comprise some sixty per cent of the population—at the
expense of the non-Muslim Indians and Chinese, who make
up most of the other forty per cent. Malays were given prefer-
ential treatment in education, business and the bureaucracy,
and Islam was promoted as a central feature of public life. The
result has been cronyism and corruption among the new Malay
élite and a lingering sense of grievance among the Indians
and the Chinese. More than half a century after independence, a sense of Malaysian, as opposed to Malay, identity has
yet to crystallise.

Meanwhile a holier-than-thou tussle has continued unabated
between UMNO and the Islamist opposition party, PAS (Parti
Islam Se-Malaysia), as to who can be trusted to safeguard the
Malays' religious and cultural heritage. I visited the northern
state of Kelantan, which borders Thailand and is a PAS stronghold. With its social conservatism and largely rural economy,
it is a far cry from high-tech Kuala Lumpur. At a crowded
meeting in an open-air market, I heard a PAS official mock the
slogan of *Islam hadari*—literally, civilisational Islam—used by
Prime Minister Abdullah Badawi to promote a modern, tolerant form of the religion. Islam is Islam, said the PAS speaker,
to the apparent delight of the audience; it needs no adjective to
define it.

A man listening to the speech told me why Kelantan needed
Islamic law: without it, there would be mixing of the sexes,
which would lead to all manner of social ills—children being
born out of wedlock, even murder. For PAS's critics, on the

other hand, its attempts to impose an Islamic puritanism have been gauche. A local spot known as 'The Beach of Passionate Love' was renamed 'Moonlight Bay'. A popular local musician was banned from playing his fiddle at weddings and concerts. PAS apparently objected to the fact that a female singer mixed with male musicians.

On my return to Kuala Lumpur, I sat with Anwar Ibrahim in his spacious home. In the course of a wide-ranging interview he made it clear that, after his years in prison, he was eager to return to the political fray. He proclaimed himself to be a good Muslim and a good democrat, committed to upholding the constitution and guaranteeing equal rights for all. He attacked rampant corruption and said that favouring the *bumiputra* had caused unacceptable inequities. But it was clear he had to strike a balance between his different constituencies—the Islamists in PAS who still hankered after some form of Islamic law, and non-Muslims apprehensive that their rights were being eroded and that they were second-class citizens.

In elections in 2008, Anwar's coalition of opposition parties won more than a third of the seats in parliament—a significant setback for UMNO and the ruling élite.[7]

* * *

At a makeshift courtroom in Jakarta, the Indonesian capital, a little old man with a wispy beard sat impassively as a witness was cross-examined. Abu Bakr Bashir was on trial for alleged involvement in the Bali bombings, two years earlier. Over 200 people, many of them Australian tourists, had been killed in suicide attacks on two of the island's nightclubs. Bashir, in his mid-sixties, was regarded as the spiritual leader of Jemaah Islamiyah, the group accused of carrying out them out.

Security was tight. Dozens of Muslim sympathisers had come to watch. One of them, an angry young student, told me

Bashir was a good Muslim who had been framed by the CIA. The old man was subsequently given a thirty-month jail term. The leniency of the sentence shocked Australians and the Bush administration in Washington. In June 2006 he walked free.[8]

With a population of some 240 million, more than eighty per cent of whom are Muslim, Indonesia is on paper the world's biggest Muslim-majority country. Yet that bald statement hides a more complex reality. Indonesians themselves make a distinction between *abangan* (nominal Muslims) and *santri* (devout Muslims). 'For all the overwhelming number of Islam's formal adherents in Indonesia,' writes one specialist, 'unambiguous Islam is a minority religion.' Indonesian Muslims view Islam in a variety of ways: they may see in it 'the central symbol of their identity, discover in it a voice of protest, or resent the sectarian demands of its zealots'. The ambiguity of Islam's political role 'has been mirrored in the ambivalence of Indonesia's rulers towards it; by and large, while trying to use it as a source of legitimacy, they have held it at arm's length'.[9]

Since the end of autocratic rule in 1998, the country has experienced over a decade of democratisation and, rather like Turkey, has been held up by some Western leaders as a role model for the rest of the Muslim world. But the shock of the Bali bombings raised unsettling questions which still persist. Is the country's traditional multi–cultural tolerance under threat? How has militant Islam taken root? And how much support does it enjoy?

A crucial factor in the spread of Islam in south-east Asia has been the role of the Muslim boarding-schools known as *pesantren*. Mostly privately funded, they number more than 10,000.[10] As with the *madrasas* of Pakistan, many teach a traditional, non-violent Islam, but others have fostered militancy and given groups of the Al-Qaeda type a toehold in the region. On the day I visited Al-Mukmin school, in the village of

Ngruki, near Solo in central Java, scrawny chickens were peck-ing at the dust in the courtyard. It was prayer time and I kicked my heels in a waiting-room where a desultory fan did nothing to dispel the heat. The school principal, Wahyuddin, had been reluctant to see me, and it wasn't hard to guess why. Set up in 1972 by the two men who went on to found Jemaah Islamiyah, Abu Bakr Bashir and Abdullah Sungkar, Al-Muk-min is widely regarded as a school for *jihad*.

The school's website says there are about 1,800 students—boys and girls, living in separate dormitories and studying in separate classrooms—and some 250 teachers and staff. There is, it says, tough discipline for all students. The main subjects are *aqidah* (Islamic creed), Shari'a (Islamic law), Arabic and English, and the school also teaches maths, science and eco-nomics. While its teaching principles are based on the Qur'an and the way of the Prophet, the website declares, in uncertain English, 'School graduates expected not trapped into fanatic mind by specific group'.[11]

Wahyuddin was distinctly defensive when at last he appeared for the interview. Neither the school nor its revered founder, Abu Bakr Bashir, were involved in terrorism. This was a lie invented by the Western media. The school had excellent rela-tions with Christians and other non-Muslims in the neighbour-hood. Nevertheless Muslims could not be passive in the face of Western aggression in the Islamic world. They could distin-guish between friends and enemies. America had imposed itself on Muslim Iraq. But there was no *jihad* against Japan.

In stark contrast to Al-Mukmin, I visited a girls' school in nearby Yogyakarta run by the Muhammadiyah—the Way of Muhammad—a movement founded in 1912 by one of the disciples of the Egyptian reformer Muhammad Abduh. The Muhammadiyah is the older of two large Muslim organisations which run networks of schools, charities and social services across the country. (The other is Nahdlatul Ulama—literally, the Awakening of the Muslim Scholars—which was founded in 1926.) The Muhammadiyah's best-known leader, Amien Rais, had been a prominent figure in the transition from dictatorship to democracy in 1998. The teenaged girls, in blue dresses and white headscarves, gave me a lively welcome. When I dropped in on an English lesson, a girl sang a Mariah Carey love song, which Abu Bakr Bashir would surely have regarded as godless decadence.

* * *

Jemaah Islamiyah is the child of an older Indonesian movement which emerged in the middle of the twentieth century. This is Darul Islam (from the Arabic *dar al-islam*, the House of Islam), whose origins lie in the country's search for a new identity after some three centuries of Dutch colonial rule. The presence of the Dutch dates from 1605, when they displaced the Portuguese from the Spice Islands (the modern-day Moluccas). Spices such as cloves, ginger, nutmeg, pepper and cinnamon were much in demand in Europe and there was intense rivalry for control of the trade. (It was only after the British failed to dislodge the Dutch from the Spice Islands that they turned their attention to India.)[12]

For most of the colonial period, the Dutch had only a tenuous hold over the Indonesian archipelago. They faced a series of rebellions not only in the Moluccas but in the two biggest islands, Java and Sumatra. They were generally disdainful of Islam and, over time, as more and more Muslims travelled to other parts of the Muslim world—for example, to perform the *hajj*, the pilgrimage to Mecca—the colonial power came to regard the religion as the source of a suspect transnational loyalty.

Java was the heart of the Dutch empire in the East, just as today it is the heart of modern Indonesia. By the mid-nineteenth century it had become hugely profitable, providing the Dutch state with a third of its revenues and making Amsterdam a major market-place for coffee, sugar and other products. The Dutch acquired a reputation in Europe, writes the historian V. G. Kiernan cryptically, as 'the most scientific of all colonial managers'.[13] Their wealth was created through the systematic exploitation of the people of Java, who not only provided forced labour but suffered periodic famine and disease, including typhoid. In the Javanese villages medical care was virtually non-existent and illiteracy widespread. By the end of the century, Dutch liberals were suffering pangs of conscience and pressed colonial administrators to introduce what became known as the 'ethical policy'. This was supposed to improve the welfare of the people. But it proved to be 'more promise than performance', and by the 1930s the policy had largely been abandoned.[14]

During the Second World War, the Dutch were ousted by the new power in Asia, the Japanese. This strengthened the desire of Indonesian nationalists to throw off the colonial yoke and, after the Japanese defeat in 1945, they declared the country independent. But the Dutch tried to re-conquer the territory, and full independence had to wait another four years. During this crucial period, Muslims and secular nationalists were at odds over the character of the new state. Those Muslims who wanted the implementation of the Shari'a (Islamic law) thought they had received a pledge to that effect, and felt betrayed when at the last minute this was dropped from the new constitution. The country's first post-independence leader, Sukarno, who was president from 1950 to 1966, was a nationalist with Marxist leanings. He committed himself to the five principles known as Pancasila. These included a belief in one God, but without giving preference to any one religion.

The feeling of Muslim betrayal animated the Darul Islam rebellion which broke out in western Java in 1948, under the leadership of the charismatic figure of Kartosuwirjo (1905–62). In 1949 Kartosuwirjo proclaimed the birth of the 'Islamic State of Indonesia', which was to be governed according to Shari'a law under his political and religious leadership. The ideology of the movement was militantly jihadist, and the initial aim of the *jihad* was to liberate the land from the Dutch. As such, it enjoyed widespread support in the villages of western Java, from where its appeal spread to other areas. By the mid-1950s, the movement may have commanded 30–40,000 armed men across the country, although many of these were only loosely aligned to Kartosuwijro. They attacked markets, cinemas and government offices, sabotaged railways and came close to assassinating President Sukarno.[15]

But once the target of the *jihad* was no longer Dutch colonial rule but the newly-independent Indonesian republic, support began to ebb away. 'In the end, [Darul Islam] was reduced to generalised terrorism, extortion and rural banditry, becoming not a model of Islamic politics but an armed plague upon the countryside.'[16] In 1962 the Indonesian army crushed the rebellion and Kartosuwirjo was captured, tried and executed by firing squad.

The spirit of Darul Islam lived on, however, both in its own right and as the progenitor of Jemaah Islamiyah. The two key figures in the emergence of Jemaah Islamiyah—Abu Bakr Bashir and Abdullah Sungkar—were both born in Java in the late 1930s into families of Yemeni descent. They became active in Darul Islam in the 1970s, during the period of its revival. In 1972 they founded Al-Mukmin school in Ngruki, and gradually the 'Ngruki network' came to acquire an identity of its own. Among their students were several of the future Bali bombers. In 1978 Bashir and Sungkar were arrested for Islamic activism by Sukarno's successor, Suharto. Suharto had taken power in the mid-1960s amid a wave of bloodshed, when as many as half a million people may have died in violence which pitted Muslims against communists.

At their trial the two men were accused of membership of Darul Islam—which they denied—and attempting to subvert the state. They were sentenced to nine years in prison but, in the event, were freed in 1982. Three years later, fearing re-arrest, they fled to Malaysia, where they set up a boarding-school in the southern state of Johor which they used to recruit and train young militants.

The 1980s were a period when the Islamic revival in the Middle East, and in particular the Khomeini revolution in Iran, had a marked impact on Indonesian Muslims. For Bashir and Sungkar and their followers, this was a crucial stage in their radicalisation. Through their involvement in the anti–Soviet war in Afghanistan, the Indonesian Islamists were able for the first time to link up with militants from the Middle East and elsewhere. It is estimated that between the mid-1980s and the early 1990s more than 500 Indonesians went to fight in the Afghan war. Many were members of Darul Islam. They included one of Bashir's most promising disciples, a young Indonesian called Riduan Isamuddin, better known as Hambali. In 1987, at the age of twenty-one, Hambali set off for Afghanistan and enrolled in one of Osama bin Laden's training camps. He became the link between Al-Qaeda and Jemaah Islamiyah.[17]

Jemaah Islamiyah (literally, the Islamic Group or Community) was formally established in Malaysia in 1993, after Bashir and Sungkar broke with Darul Islam.[18] It was distinct from the earlier movement in two important ways: it was, like Al-Qaeda, militantly Salafi in ideology and transnational in ambition. Its goal, in theory at least, was to create an Islamic caliphate centred on the whole of the Muslim archipelago stretching from southern Thailand through Indonesia to the southern Philippines. While its roots were in Indonesia and the

Darul Islam tradition, it built up an active membership in Malaysia, Singapore, the Philippines and perhaps beyond.

The movement evolved in three phases. The first, from roughly 1993 to 2000, involved patient organisation and recruitment. It is during this phase that, in 1996, Hambali and Bin Laden are believed to have formalised the link between the new organisation and Al-Qaeda. Like many Al-Qaeda 'franchises', the group enjoyed a good deal of autonomy but nevertheless looked to Bin Laden for guidance and, on occasion, assistance. The organisation received an unexpected boost in 1998 when mass demonstrations by pro-democracy activists brought about the collapse of the Suharto régime, ending more than three decades of autocratic rule. This enabled hundreds of Islamists, including Bashir and Sungkar, to return from exile. Using the Al-Mukmin school as their headquarters, they set about rebuilding the Indonesian base of their movement. The following year Sungkar died and Bashir took over as leader.

Phase two saw the start of a campaign of violence largely directed at Indonesia's Christian minority. Bashir and his followers were convinced a plot had been hatched to promote Christianity in the country as a means of undermining Islam. On Christmas Eve 2000, groups of militants under the direction of Hambali attacked some thirty-eight churches across the country, killing nineteen people. This marked Jemaah Islamiyah's coming of age, even though at the time the government in Jakarta was scarcely aware of its existence.

In the third phase, the *jihad* escalated into a campaign of attacks against Western targets. These too were masterminded by Hambali, who in late 2001 directed a group of militants to launch suicide attacks in Singapore against the US, Israeli and Australian embassies and the British High Commission, using trucks packed with ammonium nitrate. But the plot was nipped in the bud. The Singaporean authorities arrested fifteen of the plotters and, as a result, were able to piece together the first accurate assessment of Jemaah Islamiyah and its regional web. It was a sobering picture. In the words of an Australian journalist who has patiently unravelled the complex story of the organisation: 'A terrorist group with thousands of members in half a dozen countries had thrived for almost a decade, while every police force and intelligence agency in the region remained oblivious to it.'[19]

Meanwhile, undaunted by the setback in Singapore and perhaps even spurred on by it, Hambali gave orders for devastating attacks on bars and nightclubs frequented by Western tourists.

* * *

The man in overall command of Jemaah Islamiyah's most infamous and brutal operation—and the most serious attack since 9/11—was the forty-two-year-old Ali Gufron. Better known by his *nom de guerre* Mukhlas, he was born in a village in eastern Java, the eldest of three brothers, and became one of Abu Bakr Bashir's brightest pupils at the Al-Mukmin school. The field commander—in day-to-day charge of the operation—was Imam Sumudra, who had been born in Java in 1971 and was, like Mukhlas, a veteran of the Afghan war. The other key figures in the plot were Mukhlas's younger brothers, Amrozi and Ali Imron.[20]

In August 2002 the conspirators met in a village near Solo, in central Java, to lay their plans. Imam Samudra wanted to launch a spectacular attack on 11 September—the anniversary of the 9/11 attacks on New York and Washington—but it was decided there wasn't enough time. They chose as their target the island of Bali, with the deliberate intention of killing Western tourists. They also calculated that, as Bali is mainly Hindu, there would be few Muslim casualties. This was to be the group's first suicide operation, and Sumudra recruited a five-member team from whom the bombers would be drawn.

The plan went into action. Amrozi bought a white Mitsubishi van and the chemicals that were to be packed into it. In early October the plotters moved to Bali, where Samudra had rented a pink villa which was to serve as their headquarters. Here they spent anxious days mixing the chemicals and packing them into a dozen filing-cabinets. Samudra made the final selection of targets—two popular nightclubs, the Sari Club and Paddy's Bar.

In the run-up to the attacks, there were moments of black comedy. At one point the chemicals exploded because they had been packed too tightly into the filing-cabinets. The villa was filled with smoke, and for a moment the plot was in danger of being discovered. Then, on the eve of the attack, with a tonne of chemicals already loaded into the Mitsubishi van, the plotters realised that the suicide bomber who was supposed to take the van to the Sari Club couldn't drive.

But, despite these last-minute alarms, the operation went ahead on 12 October 2002. It was just after 11 p.m. on a Saturday night, and the clubs were packed. Ali Imron, with the two bombers sitting beside him, slowly drove the white van into position and then got out and walked away. The first bomber entered Paddy's Bar and in the middle of the crowded dance floor detonated a suicide-vest packed with TNT. When the panic-stricken holiday-makers rushed out into the street, the second bomber blew up the van. The carnage was horrific. Two hundred and two people were killed and another 350 seriously wounded. The dead included eighty-eight Australians, thirty-eight Indonesians (Muslim and non-Muslim) and twenty-four Britons.

***

Terrible as the bombings were, they could have been worse. The chemicals had been poorly mixed, which weakened the impact of the main bomb. And it turned out that Amrozi had failed to remove a tell-tale identification number from the chassis of the van. He was arrested and, after twenty-four hours of interrogation, confessed. Other arrests followed and, within three months of the bombings, the cell responsible for them had been dismantled. In 2003 Hambali was captured in Thailand and handed over to the Americans, who held him in Guantanamo Bay, refusing to allow the Indonesian authorities access to him.

But despite the shock of the bombings, the Indonesian government was reluctant to outlaw Jemaah Islamiyah, fearing this would provoke a Muslim backlash. Al-Mukmin school—unlike its Malaysian counterpart—was not shut down. This led to friction between Indonesian officials and their American and Australian allies. There was also outrage among the victims' families at what was seen as the lenient sentence eventually handed down, after a series of trials, to Abu Bakr Bashir.

Other suicide bombings followed: an attack on the Marriott hotel in Jakarta in 2003, which killed eleven people, all but one of them Indonesians; the bombing of the Australian embassy in the capital in 2004, which killed eleven Indonesians; and the second Bali bombings in 2005, which killed twenty people, fifteen of them Indonesians. All this put mounting pressure on the authorities to act. There were moments when they seemed, in public at least, to be in denial over the existence of a home-grown *jihadi* movement linked to Al-Qaeda. But behind the scenes they were more active than this suggested. With the help of money and expertise from Australia and the United States, they embarked on much-needed reform of the police and set up a de-radicalisation programme designed to draw militants away from extremism.[21]

In November 2008, six years after the event, the three men convicted of planning and carrying out the first Bali bombings—Imam Sumudra and the two brothers Mukhlas and Amrozi—were executed by firing squad. (The third brother, Ali Imron, had repented and been spared.) While many Indonesians felt justice had been done, there were some who regarded the executed men as martyrs.

* * *

The young woman behind the bar in a dingy suburb of Jakarta told me what had happened one night in Ramadan, the Muslim month of fasting. At around eight o'clock, the police had arrived to warn her that a group of vigilantes were going to smash up the bar. A few hours later, hundreds of men turned up in trucks and on motor-bikes, trashed the place and then went on down the street doing the same to other bars. The police not only knew what was happening, they knew who was responsible and did nothing.

Later, at a smart hotel downtown, I sat and talked to Hilmy Bakr Almascaty, one of the leaders of the group that carried out the attacks, the Islamic Defenders' Front. He was young, single-minded and unrepentant. Those who wanted to drink, he said, could do so for eleven months of the year, but not in the month of fasting. He made it clear that any bar or restaurant serving alcohol during Ramadan was a legitimate target.

The front is not just a group of thugs, but a new force on the political scene. Set up in 1998, it has allies in the government and the police who turn a blind eye to its violent activities. It was among the radical groups which in 2008 hounded the country's Ahmadi minority. Public opinion, previously indulgent towards the front, was aghast when its members beat up peaceful demonstrators at a rally in the capital in support of religious freedom. The front's tolerated existence, and

161

that of other radical groups such as Hizb ut-Tahrir, which has a growing following on Indonesian campuses, raises questions about where south-east Asia is heading. Moreover the bombing of two hotels in Jakarta in July 2009 showed that, although weakened and fragmented, Jemaah Islamiyah was not a spent force.

Is the region's traditional multi–cultural tolerance under threat? The evidence is mixed. Indonesia's two largest Muslim movements, the Muhammadiyah and Nahdlatul Ulama, claim a membership of thirty-five million and forty million, respectively (figures that are admittedly hard to verify). Jemaah Islamiyah probably has a hard core of a few hundred and a support network of a few thousand. There are nevertheless anxious policy-makers in all the region's capitals. One of the most candid assessments I heard of their collective security concerns was not in predominantly Muslim Indonesia but in Manila, capital of the staunchly Catholic Philippines.

South-east Asia's intrinsic problem, said José Almonte, was that it had 'large Muslim communities and weak secular governments'. General Almonte had been national security adviser to President Fidel Ramos for much of the 1990s. As such, he had been closely involved in efforts to end the long-running Muslim insurgency in the southern Philippines. Now retired, he had become one of the region's elder statesmen.[22] He handed me a copy, fresh from the printing-press, of a collection of his lectures and writings entitled *Toward One Southeast Asia*. The foreword had been written, from jail, by Anwar Ibrahim. In a section on the 'war on terrorism' the general declared: 'At bottom, Islamism is a rebellion of the *excluded* ... That is why— like many other poor countries sympathetic to the anti–terrorist coalition's cause—we in the Philippines believe the global community must look beyond the war on terrorism—and deal once and for all with the inequities spurring it.'[23]

General Almonte was a loyal ally of the United States, but not an uncritical one. He thought its response to the extremist threat had at times been misguided. The invasion of Iraq, in particular, had inflamed Muslim sentiment in Asia as well as the Middle East. He wanted the region's governments and its collective body, the Association of Southeast Asian Nations (ASEAN), to work together more effectively against the challenge of radical Islam. He made a distinction between the response of strong states—Singapore and Malaysia—and that of 'their relatively weaker counterparts in Indonesia and the Philippines'.

The threat of jihadism in the Muslim archipelago has receded but not disappeared. The region's traditional multi–cultural tolerance is alive but not unscathed.

8

THE BOMB IN THE TURBAN

On a bright spring day, the great and the good from Europe and the Muslim world gathered in a Sussex manor in a condition close to despair. 'There is no trust,' lamented a senior Muslim diplomat, contemplating the torn relations between Europe and Islam. 'Dialogue has failed. We need a historic reconciliation.' No one seemed inclined to contradict him.

The event brought together government ministers, diplomats, academics, journalists and human-rights activists to consider the fall-out from the 'cartoon affair'. The publication in 2005 of cartoons depicting the Prophet Muhammad—the most infamous of them showing a bomb in his turban—provoked a wave of Muslim anger around the world. The cartoons first appeared in Denmark's biggest-circulation daily, *Jyllands-Posten*, a conservative paper with close links to the government of the day. A few months later they were reprinted in newspapers in several other European countries. While in Europe the protests were largely peaceful, in the Middle East, Pakistan and Nigeria demonstrations turned violent and dozens were killed.[1]

The cartoon affair had a deeply polarising effect, encouraging Muslims and non-Muslims to think the worst of one another. Non-Muslims saw the protests as proof that Muslims were hostile to freedom of expression and other liberal values and all too prone to violence. Muslims saw the publication and re-publication of the cartoons as a deliberate affront to their Prophet, their faith and themselves. The none-too-subtle message of the bomb in the turban was that Muslim violence was the product not of a small radical fringe but of Islam itself. What was so offensive to Muslims was the direct, unequivocal link between the Prophet and violent extremism. A Muslim political leader in Turkey declared that the affair 'revealed once again Europe's true face as an enemy of the East and Islam ... Animosity towards Islam is in the genes of the West ... Europe displays its hatred and vengeance ... at every available opportunity'.[2]

The controversy was in several respects a re-run of the Rushdie affair of the late 1980s (which I describe in more detail below). Both involved a perceived insult to the Prophet, hence arousing strong feelings among the devout as well as among activists, and both were hijacked for political ends. *The Satanic Verses* affair had been exploited by the Iranian leader Ayatollah Khomeini, whose death threat against Rushdie and his publishers was a means of asserting his authority in the Muslim world. The cartoon affair was used by Muslim leaders in Europe, the Middle East and elsewhere to whip up a storm and thereby promote themselves and their causes. In each case a local crisis was internationalised, which both complicated its resolution and tended to eclipse the original sense of Muslim grievance.[3]

The cartoon affair was one of Europe's 'culture wars'. If the issue was not a novel or a cartoon, it was the headscarf or the *burqa* or a Mozart opera or remarks about Islam by Pope Benedict or the Archbishop of Canterbury. The media loved these rows, and often sensationalised them. In a sense, the cartoon affair was a microcosm of the rift between Islam and the West. Moreover it was a quarrel between peoples rather than governments. To the dismay of the leaders meeting at the Sussex manor, it had acquired a grass-roots dynamic beyond their control. One could see this in the way newspaper columnists, on both sides of the divide, let rip—and in the way housewives in the oil-rich Arab states of the Gulf boycotted Danish milk and butter. The crisis unleashed deep emotions in two sets of protagonists who were both convinced they were right. It was a clash of self-righteousness which raised troubling questions about the prospects for integrating fifteen million Muslims into the secular societies of western Europe.

* * *

Muslims have lived in Europe for centuries but only began to form sizeable communities in the 1950s and 1960s, when a growing number migrated to countries that were rebuilding themselves after the destruction of the Second World War. They were ethnically diverse: Turks and Kurds came to Germany, Pakistanis and Bangladeshis to Britain, Algerians and Moroccans to France. Islam was part of who they were, but not necessarily the dominant part. They had few skills, providing cheap labour for factories, mines and mills. They worked long hours and frequently experienced illness, poverty and discrimination.

At first they were scarcely visible: they tended not to speak the local languages or mix very much with the local people or make demands on the host societies. Many clung to the 'myth of return', believing that once they had made enough money they would return home to lead prosperous lives. But when the labour shortage eased and European states began to set limits on immigration, this first generation of working men hastened to bring over their wives and children while they still had the chance. Once they started putting down roots, everything changed. Muslim families had new needs—for mosques and schools and some sort of recognition of their holidays and traditions. In the eyes of the non-Muslim majority, they were transformed over time from a cultural presence to a political problem and, increasingly after 9/11, to the 'enemy within'.[4]

There were a number of turning-points. For the French, it was the headscarf affair; for the Dutch, the killing of the film-maker Theo van Gogh; for the British, the drama that erupted in the late 1980s over Salman Rushdie's novel *The Satanic Verses*. Muslims had been a growing presence in Britain for three or four decades, but most Britons were scarcely aware of them. To be sure, there had been a precursor to the Rushdie affair in the Yorkshire city which was to become its epicentre. This was the Honeyford affair. Ray Honeyford was a Bradford head teacher who took exception to the liberal policies—known collectively as multi–culturalism—which successive British governments had endorsed since the 1960s. The heart of these policies is the rejection of an imposed assimilation in favour of voluntary integration and the acceptance of diversity. In Honeyford's eyes, this was a form of political correctness which gave undue autonomy to minorities who did not accept the British way of life. Since sixteen per cent of Bradford's population are Muslim—originally, for the most part, from villages in Pakistani–controlled Kashmir—and many of the city's state schools are predominantly Asian, Honeyford found himself at loggerheads with a community which saw him as the enemy. Following sustained protests, he was eventually forced into early retirement.[5]

But this was a little local difficulty compared with what followed. Salman Rushdie's novel was published in September 1988 and, although few Muslims read it, the word soon spread among Bradford Muslims that the author—originally from a Muslim family in Bombay—was an apostate who had slandered the Prophet. In January 1989 the Bradford Council for Mosques organised a protest at which the book was publicly burned; it even filmed the protestors doing so. The affair had an instantly polarising effect, just as the Danish cartoon affair did a decade and a half later. Hitherto British society, especially in the metropolis, had paid little attention to the growing Muslim communities living in its midst, in run-down parts of inner cities such as the old East End of London and the industrial centres of the Midlands, northern England and Glasgow. Now politicians, intellectuals and the media were made rudely aware of this Muslim presence and saw it in a wholly unfavourable light. Muslims were depicted as book-burners and bigots and enemies of freedom of expression.

After the book-burning the *Yorkshire Post* denounced the protestors as 'intellectual hooligans' and compared them to Nazis.[6] National newspapers took a similar line. The *Independent* declared that in burning Rushdie's book Muslims were 'following the example of the Inquisition and Hitler's National Socialists'. In an editorial, the newspaper paid tribute to Muslims' 'devotion to family values, hard work and personal integrity', adding that 'their spiritual values should be respected, and ... they should be spared from racial discrimination in all its forms'. But the paper's conclusion was unequivocal: 'They in turn, however, must not seek to impose their values either on their fellow Britons of other faiths or on the majority who acknowledge no faith at all.'[7]

Roy Hattersley, a Labour MP in a multi–cultural Birmingham constituency, sought to challenge the consensus. 'Every group within our society must obey the law,' he declared. 'But support for that principle is not the same as insisting that "they" must behave like "us". The doctrine of assimilation is arrogant and patronising ... In a free society the Muslim community must be allowed to do what it likes to do as long as the choice it makes is not damaging to the community as a whole.' But this was a distinctly minority view, widely denounced as appeasement of Muslim 'fanatics'.[8]

For their part, Muslims rallied behind a cause which brought them together—young and old, members of rival sects, the more religious and the more secular—in a new way. They saw the book, just as they were later to see the Danish cartoons, as a deliberate assault. The polarisation between Muslim and non-Muslim was acute, but largely localised until February 1989—five months after the novel's publication—when the Iranian leader Ayatollah Khomeini issued his infamous *fatwa*, or ruling, condemning Rushdie and his publishers to death. On this, Muslims were far more divided, with only a militant few openly supporting the death sentence. But the damage had been done; the affair had been internationalised. Now Muslims were not merely book-burners opposed to the central tenets of a liberal society but murderers or potential murderers. Some of the protests turned violent. Rushdie was put under police protection. Britain broke off diplomatic relations with Tehran and the affair further poisoned relations between Islam and the West.

The Rushdie affair had two important effects. It dramatised the new Muslim presence in Britain, which in half a century had grown from 21,000 to about a million and was now viewed not in purely local terms but as an unwelcome part of the global Islamic resurgence. In this sense, Khomeini's *fatwa* implanted in the public mind the idea that Muslims living in the West were susceptible to radical influences from the Middle East and were therefore a fifth column. A second consequence, although this only became fully apparent later, was that the affair led a highly diverse set of Muslim communities in Britain to begin to feel they were a national community. What brought them together was a shared perception that they had to defend their faith and their identity against the hostility of British society and the British media. In time, the anti–Rushdie movement grew into the first national body of British Muslim organisations, the Muslim Council of Britain. Painful and divisive as it was, the Rushdie affair marked the coming of age of British Islam.

* * *

Around the same time, the headscarf affair ignited in France, home to the largest Muslim community in western Europe, numbering today some five million (about eight per cent of the population). France's approach to cultural diversity is very different from Britain's. Its notion of secularism, or *laïcité*, is based on a history of opposition between the state and the Catholic church which has resulted—in theory at least—in the strict separation of religion and state. According to French Republican values, religion should be kept out of the public sphere and in particular from state schools, seen as factories of secular civic virtues. 'Communalism'—as promoted by British-style multi–culturalism—is viewed as a threat to national identity and national unity.

Seen in this light, the settlement of increasing numbers of Muslims, mainly from France's former colonies in North Africa, opened up old wounds. Politically speaking, the presence of a large number of Algerians and their French-born descendants—the single biggest group of Muslims—was a constant reminder of a painful page in French history. Moreover, in demanding the right to attend state schools wearing headscarves, Muslims of North African origin were seen as threatening *laïcité*, one of the cornerstones of French national life.

The headscarf affair is puzzling to outsiders.[9] It began in 1989 when three girls in Creil, a town near Paris, were expelled from school because they insisted on wearing headscarves, and it continued on and off for a decade and a half. The affair underlined the new visibility and assertiveness of Europe's Muslims. The schoolgirls at the heart of the controversy were, like the young anti–Rushdie protestors in Britain, second-generation Muslims. What startled many in France, not least feminists who saw the girls as victims of Muslim male oppression, was that many of them were articulate and self-confident. While some may indeed have been subjected to social pressures to cover their heads, many clearly had not. Their motives were mixed and not always easy to discern. Some wore the headscarf as a religious duty, others as a mark of identity and adolescent self-assertion and still others—by no means the majority—as a badge of Islamism.

The affair rumbled on, under different governments, until finally President Jacques Chirac appointed two commissions whose work led to the passage of a new law in 2004 which banned 'ostentatious' religious symbols in state schools. In the end, after all the sound and fury, the number of girls excluded for refusing to observe the law was relatively small. The symbolism of the affair was nevertheless considerable. Behind a small piece of cloth lay a host of stated and unstated anxieties about the new Muslim presence; anxieties the new law could mask but not allay.[10]

* * *

Nabil arrives at my hotel beside a canal in Amsterdam wearing a smart brown suit. He is a taxi driver who has spent half his twenty-six years in Morocco and the other half in the Netherlands. He speaks fluent Dutch, English and Arabic.

Nabil becomes my guide to Islam in Amsterdam. He takes me to the district where he used to live, one of the city's predominantly Muslim suburbs, a drab area of apartment blocks, Turkish kebab houses and Moroccan cafés. The Netherlands is home to about a million Muslims, out of a population of some sixteen million. The two biggest communities—roughly equal in numbers—are the Turks and the Moroccans. As Nabil explains, they have little to do with one another, preferring to frequent their own mosques, youth clubs and community centres. The Turks, he says with a touch of irony, are a mutual-welfare society. The Moroccans, by implication, are not; they are divided between city-dwelling Arabs like Nabil's family, who are from Rabat, and the more numerous Berbers from the villages of the Atlas mountains, whose transposition to the cold, secular cities of northern Europe caused profound culture shock.

This is the suburb where a young Dutch-Moroccan called Muhammad Bouyeri grew up. Nabil remembers him as a pretty typical second-generation kid. He went to a good school—which described him as a 'B-level student'—and at first seemed to integrate reasonably well into Dutch society. But then he drifted into crime and spent seven months in jail. He broke with his father. He had difficulty finding a girlfriend. Then, on top of everything, his mother died of cancer. After a period of depression he became a born-again Muslim and fell under the influence of a radical Syrian *imam*. He became an active member of what the Dutch security forces came to call the Hofstad group, which had links with foreign jihadists and apparently planned to carry out attacks in Dutch cities.

On 2 November 2004, the twenty-six–year-old Bouyeri shot Theo van Gogh—a controversial film-maker and relative of the famous painter—as he was cycling along an Amsterdam street. He then cut his throat and pinned to his body a wild, rambling note seeking to justify his action. The horrific killing plunged a small, traditionally liberal country into a crisis marked by intense soul-searching and sharp polarisation.[11]

'After that,' said Nabil, 'people looked at you differently.' Virtually every young Moroccan I met told me the same story. After the killing and the wave of shock and recrimination that followed, all Muslims came under a cloud of suspicion. Anyone who looked Moroccan would be challenged—at college, in a shop, on the tram, in the street—to condemn or condone the killing. We condemned it, Nabil told me—but why were we somehow made to feel responsible for it?

Van Gogh had, to be sure, been controversial—a professional *provocateur* who, after attacking Christians and Jews on his television show, turned his fire on Muslims—whom he routinely called 'goat-fuckers'. Together with another controversial figure, the Somali–born Dutch politician Ayaan Hirsi Ali, he had made a film called *Submission*, which depicted Islam and the Qur'an as brutally oppressive of women. This had apparently been the last straw for Bouyeri. 'I acted out of faith,' he declared at his trial. It was his duty, he said, speaking in Dutch, to 'cut off the heads of all those who insult Allah and his Prophet'. And he went on: 'You can send all your psychologists and all your psychiatrists, and all your experts, but I'm telling you, you will never understand. You cannot understand. And I'm telling you, if I had the chance to be freed and the chance to repeat what I did on the second of November, *wallahi* [by Allah] I'm telling you, I would do exactly the same.'[12]

Bouyeri was sentenced to life in jail. His court appearance—a self-assured young Muslim, born and bred in the Netherlands, calmly justifying a particularly brutal murder in the name of his faith—made a powerful impression on Dutch public opinion. As in Britain, multi–culturalism became suspect.

* * *

Lale is a young German Muslim who wears a bright pink headscarf. Although she studied law, she has had to take a job in a call-centre. She would like something better, but employers think the headscarf will put off their customers. 'It's very difficult,' she tells me. 'You never really feel part of society.'

Lale is one of Germany's 3.3 million Muslims (about four per cent of the population). Most—about three-quarters—are, like her, of Turkish descent. In Britain and France, Muslim immigration has a colonial context. In Germany it is the result of bilateral agreements in the early 1960s which enabled employers to recruit hundreds of thousands of Turkish workers. The authorities termed them *gastarbeiter* (guest workers), on the grounds that Germany was not a country of immigration and had no desire to see their long-term settlement. But, as elsewhere in Europe, the numbers grew rapidly: from about half a million in 1971 to one and a half million in 1981.[13]

The issues that make headlines in Germany are the same as those elsewhere in Europe—headscarves, 'honour' killings, education, unemployment, security fears—but at the same time the country has its own characteristics which set it apart from its neighbours. Crucial among them is a concept of 'Germanness' based on blood and ethnicity, which has meant that for most of the last four decades immigrants from Turkey have found it hard to gain German citizenship.

Another distinctive German feature is the *Bundesamt für Verfassungsschutz*, the Federal Office for the Protection of the Constitution. The rough equivalent of Britain's MI5 and the American FBI, this organisation monitors extremists, including Islamist groups. Claudia Schmid, who runs its Berlin branch, told me why even non-violent Islamists are deemed to be a threat. 'Our task is to inform the public and the state institutions about groups which are trying to change the fundamental values of our constitution. These groups can function and promote their ideas. But they can't expect to get money from the state if they want to destroy essential, fundamental elements of our constitution.'

The *Verfassungsschutz*—which is part of the Ministry of the Interior—keeps a close eye on Islamist groups such as the Muslim Brotherhood and its Turkish counterpart, Milli Görüş. As Lale discovered, to belong to these groups or even associate with them is to risk being denied German citizenship or access to official funding. When she is not at the call-centre, she is a volunteer worker with a Muslim youth group. Because it worked with Arab and Turkish Islamists, its state funding was cut off. 'We are doing a good job,' Lale told me. 'The problem is that there is always suspicion from the politicians. They say: we like your projects—but can we really trust you?'

Trust, or lack of it, lies at the heart of the problem. A citizenship test introduced in the state of Baden-Württemberg is popularly known as the 'Muslim test'. Erkan Arikan, a journalist of Turkish descent, told me about one particularly sensitive question. 'You've found your son is homosexual and he comes to you and says, "Dad, I want to marry a German homosexual guy." So how do you react? Do they expect that I will beat up my son, or do a kind of 'honour' killing? This is really ridiculous.'

Since 9/11 Germany has not suffered an attack by global jihadists, but there have been some near misses. In September 2007 the authorities announced they had foiled a 'massive' attack on American military facilities in the country. They had arrested two German converts to Islam and a Turkish citizen, all of them young men in their twenties who had trained in camps in Pakistan. The 'Sauerland cell', as the media called it, had gathered enough explosives for bombings that, according to officials, would have been 'worse than London or Madrid'.[14]

This heightened fears that Muslims posed a threat to security, as well as to social cohesion, and made it harder for German society to come to terms with the Muslim presence in its midst. Nevertheless an initiative taken by the government in September 2006 suggested official attitudes might slowly be changing. This was the German Conference on Islam, a high-profile event launched in Berlin by the Minister of the Interior,

Wolfgang Schäuble, which brought together state officials and representatives of the main Muslim organisations. A young Muslim academic, Rim Spielhaus, daughter of an Egyptian father and an East German mother and a member of one of the working groups set up by the conference, told me it was an essential first step. 'The Interior Minister started the conference by proclaiming that Muslims are part of Germany. I think that was an important signal that we hadn't had for forty years.'

* * *

Shamsul sits on his sofa in a modest house on the edge of Leeds, a proud father cradling his six–month-old son. Like many journalists, I have made the pilgrimage from London to Leeds in the wake of the suicide bombings which shook the British capital on 7 July 2005, when four young Muslims targeted trains on the London Underground and a double-decker bus, killing fifty-six people including themselves.

In the decade and a half since the Rushdie affair, Britain's Muslim population had grown to 1.6 million (about three per cent of the population). According to confidential government figures, it was among the country's most disadvantaged minorities: 'Compared with the population as a whole Muslims have three times the unemployment rate (15%); the lowest economic activity rates (48%); a higher proportion of unqualified citizens (43%); and a higher concentration in deprived areas (15%).'[15]

Radical Islamists had been building up a presence in Europe throughout the 1980s and 1990s. London in particular had become a sanctuary for Islamist *émigrés* from Saudi Arabia, Egypt, Algeria and elsewhere, and had as a result been dubbed 'Londonistan'.[16] Europe had been a base rather than a target: the attacks of 9/11, for example, had been planned by an Al-Qaeda cell in Hamburg. There had been a belief among policy-makers and security officials that Europe was so useful to the jihadists—as a place to raise money, find recruits, make propaganda or just lie low—that it was not in their interests to attack its cities.

This illusion was shattered by the Madrid train bombings of 11 March 2004, which killed 191 people and wounded 1,800. Coming only a few days before a Spanish election, the attacks served to oust a conservative prime minister and give victory to a centre-left government which immediately announced the withdrawal of the country's troops from Iraq: an extraordinary coup for the bombers. Whether the attacks were the work of Al-Qaeda, however, was not clear; there was suspicion but no solid proof. Two American counter-terror experts concluded that the bombings were an *homage* to Al-Qaeda, demonstrating 'the global reach of bin Laden's ideas, not his operations'.[17]

Then the following year came the London bombings, carried out by four young Muslims—their average age twenty-two—who had been born and bred in Britain. Shamsul had grown up with three of them in Beeston, a predominantly Pakistani suburb of Leeds. 'You could have left your house keys with them and gone away for a year,' he told me. 'You could have trusted them with everything you had.'

What about the leader of the group, a thirty-year-old local teacher called Muhammad Siddique Khan? Was Shamsul puzzled by what he'd done? 'It doesn't puzzle me at all,' he replied. 'He was a smart, intelligent young man—and to carry out the sort of actions that he did, you'd have to be quite smart. It probably took years of planning and preparation. So in that respect I admire him—to have the courage and determination to carry out what he did. But I also totally disagree with the actions themselves, because there are, in this country particularly, more peaceful, democratic means of self-expression.'[18]

So what had motivated Khan? In Shamsul's view, the answer was to be found in his posthumous video. This was issued, and presumably produced, by Al-Qaeda. Somehow Khan's mournful Yorkshire accent made the familiar jihadist message more chilling: 'I and thousands like me have forsaken everything for what we believe. Our driving motivation doesn't come from tangible commodities that this world has to offer. Our religion is Islam, obedience to the one true God, Allah …

'Your democratically-elected governments,' he went on, 'continuously perpetrate atrocities against my people all over the world, and your support of them makes you directly responsible—just as I am responsible for protecting and avenging my Muslim brothers and sisters. And until you stop the bombing, gassing, imprisonment and torture of my people, we will not stop this fight.' He added: 'We are at war and I am a soldier. Now you too will taste the reality of this situation.'

The British people had *not*, of course, supported their government's decision to attack Iraq in 2003; far from it. But in jihadist logic, those who vote for a government in a Western democracy become responsible for its actions. In Shamsul's view, Khan and his colleagues had been radicalised by British foreign policy towards Palestine, Afghanistan and, above all, Iraq. He regarded the tape as a credible explanation of their actions.

Khan seemed to epitomise the new home-grown *jihadi*—a young man who had had a good education, seemed to get on well with his non-Muslim peers (who nicknamed him 'Sid') and became a respected teacher in his local community. He had taken part in a campaign to get young people off drugs. He was in some respects integrated into British society, and yet so profoundly alienated from it that he was prepared to kill his fellow citizens, apparently as payback for Britain's role in Iraq and elsewhere.[19]

If there was uncertainty about Al-Qaeda involvement in the Madrid bombings, it was equally unclear—at least at first—whether it was behind the London attacks. But evidence gradually came to light of a connection between Khan and the Al-Qaeda leadership in Pakistan ('Al-Qaeda Central', as it had become known). Khan had been to Pakistan, stayed at a *madrasa* with known radical links and reportedly contacted Al-Qaeda people there. The planner of the London bombings was identified as Abu Ubaida al-Masri, an Egyptian who had fought in Afghanistan and become an explosives expert for Al-Qaeda, losing two fingers in the process.[20] British officials warned that because of the strong links between Britain's Muslims and Pakistan future attacks were likely; indeed many experts saw Britain as the most vulnerable country in Europe.

The London bombings had far-reaching domestic repercussions. First, the New Labour government of Tony Blair—unwilling to publicly acknowledge any link between Iraq and radicalisation—sought to co-opt Muslim religious and community leaders in a new campaign against extremism. This had only limited success. Muslim leaders were ready to condemn terrorism but remained wary of a government whose forces were fighting Muslims in Iraq and Afghanistan, and which had tied itself so closely to America's 'war on terror'. Second, the bombings prompted a wave of soul-searching about whether British multi-culturalism had failed, with a chorus of voices concluding it had, and a beleaguered minority pointing out that the number of extremists was very small and that a great many Muslims were, largely unnoticed, integrating into British society.

* * *

On a freezing winter day, I took the Metro and then a train from the heart of Paris to the outer suburb of Clichy-sous-Bois. Here, a few months earlier, in October 2005, two French Muslim teenagers had been accidentally killed while running from the police—an event which had sparked weeks of riots by angry young Muslims, mostly from Arab or African families, who clashed with police, burnt cars and damaged property.

At a local youth club, auditions were under way for budding stand-up comedians. One young woman, Fifu, was performing a sketch poking fun at life in a traditional French-Algerian family. A lively twenty-something who chooses not to cover her head, Fifu told me about the routine. 'This is about my family of eight children. They ask their father to go out on Saturday night. They understand the traditional ways that their father tried to teach them. And at the same time they would like to go out and have boyfriends and girlfriends. They want everything. They want the original traditions and they want to have [the] modern pleasures of teenagers.'[21]

Satire was a way of expressing the frustrations of being children of two cultures. But the riots had shown that those frustrations ran deep. The problems of the suburbs—crime, drugs, unemployment, severe tensions between the youth and the police—had festered for years. Muhammad, an articulate young social worker born and bred in the suburbs, told me of the daily frustrations. 'Three ID checks a day! The first one you say yes—the second one you are angry—the third, it's hard not to blow a fuse.'

I walked with Muhammad through the suburb where he had grown up, past a shop offering cheap phone calls to the Arab world, Turkey and Pakistan, to an open-air market selling food and clothes along with prayer mats and cassettes of the Qur'an. We passed a police station which had been burnt down. I asked Muhammad where home was, and he looked at me in surprise. 'These streets are my home,' he said with obvious pride. As for the Champs Elysées and the bright lights of downtown Paris, they were a world away.

* * *

Nabil liked jazz, and it was to the accompaniment of Louis Armstrong that he drove me one day from Amsterdam to The Hague. Our first stop was the modern parliament building, to meet Nebahat Albayrak, a Turkish-born woman in her late thirties and one of seven Muslim members of the Dutch parliament (most fairly nominal Muslims but a significant number nevertheless). She is a politician of the centre-left and a year after our meeting became one of the first two Muslims to become junior ministers in a Dutch government (the other was a well-known Dutch-Moroccan figure, Ahmed Aboutaleb).

When I asked her whether the Dutch model of integration had failed, she replied, 'We have never seriously accepted the fact that we are an immigration country.' In the 1970s and 1980s the official approach was liberal and well-intentioned, and large sums of money were spent on efforts to integrate minorities. But the attitude, she said, was not so much one of tolerance as indifference. 'Generations were growing up with the message: "Don't think you are staying here—we don't really have to invest in you—[because] we don't think that you belong here." And so the children that the first generation raised have been in the Netherlands with only one foot—the other foot was either in Turkey or in Morocco. And somehow I see around me now young people who don't feel at home in their country.'[22]

I left her office wondering what happens to these young Muslims who don't feel they belong. Down the road from the parliament, at the As-Sunnah mosque, I found one possible answer. Like many of Europe's mosques, it's tucked away in a dull, featureless part of town, beside a car wash. I had heard that the mosque was attracting young people in large numbers and wanted to know why.

The message of the Syrian *imam*, Sheikh Fawwaz, is simple and uncompromising. 'Islam is one,' he told me, speaking in Arabic. 'And we want to teach it just as it was revealed by the Prophet Muhammad—not any other Islam.' This is the Salafi Islam I had encountered in Saudi Arabia and Pakistan, rooted in a desire to return to the original purity of the faith. Sheikh Fawwaz's mosque is conservative and, unlike those I had visited in Amsterdam, multi–ethnic. In the corridor outside the sheikh's office I talked to young people with family roots in Somalia, Morocco and Turkey. I asked one young Turkish Kurd why he didn't go to a mosque where he would find a Turkish rather than an Arab *imam*. He said he preferred the As-Sunnah mosque because there were a lot of *shabab* (young men) like him and because he respected Sheikh Fawaaz for his Islamic learning.

I asked the sheikh if he believed in integration. 'The problem with integration,' he replied, 'is that, like many other Western concepts, we're never told what it involves. It can lead to the oppression of Muslims. People want Muslim women to take off the *hijab* [headscarf] and Muslim men to shave off our beards. All this is done in the name of integration. In my view these are personal choices; they've got nothing to do with integration. People don't say it openly, but they want Muslims to abandon vital aspects of our faith and culture.'

It was an ambivalent response and, as we left, I wondered what Nabil—the jazz-loving Dutch-Moroccan taxi driver—thought of the sheikh and the mosque. His reaction took me by surprise. 'I felt a kind of brotherhood,' he said. 'They gave me the feeling that I'm one of them.' As for the influence of the sheikh on the young: 'He speaks clearly about the questions the youth have. He's got answers—simple answers—but that's exactly what the youth need: a person who gives them the right direction.'

The mosque has had a bad press. Dutch journalists see it as a hotbed of Saudi–style Wahhabism, and there have been allegations of links to extremism—though no hard evidence I could discover. Salafism remains a small current within Dutch (and European) Islam but, given its appeal to the disoriented young, it looks set to grow.

* * *

Over the last two decades a series of crises and controversies, from the Rushdie affair to the Madrid and London bombings and the Danish cartoons, have kept alive a sharply polarised debate about the new Muslim presence in Europe and its implications. Shaping that debate has been the fact that two distinct agendas—one focused on integration and the other on security—have become inextricably intertwined. There is a widespread view, inside and outside Europe, that the continent has wholly failed to integrate its new Muslims. This in turn is deemed to be producing a degree of alienation and radicalisation among Muslim youth that is threatening the security not only of Europe but of the United States, which faces the danger that young Muslims with clean European passports will come and carry out some future attack.[23]

This view may be unduly alarmist. It ignores the fact that integration is a daily reality—patchy and incomplete, to be sure, but a reality nevertheless. Those who have conducted serious research on the subject reject the idea that integration is not happening or that Muslims are uniquely resistant to it.[24] Moreover, to look at the new and permanent Muslim presence in Europe through the narrow lens of security is at best to distort a complex reality and at worst to succumb to the politics of fear. There is an inescapable contradiction between telling law-abiding, hard-working Muslims that they are welcome as fellow citizens and at the same time putting their mosques under surveillance, badgering them to change their behaviour in personal and family matters, and tightening up counter-terror legislation to the point where civil liberties are eroded. Europe may indeed be Islam's new frontier. It is also an important case study in multi–cultural coexistence.

9

HEARTS AND MINDS

Sitting in his office at the Rand Corporation—part of that sprawling complex of security-related organisations on the edge of Washington which advise and work with the Pentagon—Bruce Hoffman does not mince his words. 'We've lost the current generation of [Al-Qaeda] terrorists. We're probably on the verge of losing the next generation. And that's why we have to harness our efforts on the generation after next.'[1]

Hoffman speaks with authority, as one of America's foremost experts on terrorism who began thinking about the link between religion and political violence long before it was fashionable to do so. He believes that, after 9/11, the Bush administration was slow to realise that the 'war on terror' could not be won by military means alone.

In October 2003 Bush's Defence Secretary, Donald Rumsfeld, wrote a memo to his aides. 'Are we winning or losing the Global War on Terror?' he asked. 'Are we capturing, killing or deterring and dissuading more terrorists every day than the *madrasas* and the radical clerics are recruiting, training and deploying against us? Does the US need to fashion a broad, integrated plan to stop the next generation of terrorists?'[2]

He was at least asking the right questions. But it is not evident that he or his colleagues produced the right answers. Experts such as Hoffman argue that, like the Cold War, this new war has an ideological dimension which requires the sophisticated use of the tools of 'soft power' (diplomacy, intelligence, propaganda, economic aid and so on). But there is an important difference between the Cold War and the 'war on terror'. In the confrontation between NATO and the Warsaw Pact, America was essentially fighting governments: the people were allies, or potential allies. Now, it is the other way round: America finds itself allied with unpopular Muslim governments against a radical Islamism which draws support from the people. This is a much weaker position from which to wage a struggle for hearts and minds.

Even when Bush and his senior officials began to acknowledge the ideological component of the struggle, they did so without a discernible strategy. There were those who adopted the Madison Avenue approach: America had a bad image in the Muslim world and dollars could buy it a better one. At the other end of the spectrum there were those who advocated nothing less than a campaign of social engineering in Muslim countries—an approach which at times seemed to echo the old colonial 'civilising mission'.[3]

Some, led by the president himself, saw democracy as the antidote to terror. But the failure to turn Iraq into the shining city on the hill did much to discredit this idea and, in any case, in his second term Bush effectively abandoned the 'freedom agenda'. Some saw the eradication of poverty, disease and illiteracy as an essential task in pulling the rug from under the jihadists; others thought this irrelevant.[4] Experts were divided over which term to use (hearts and minds, war of ideas, outreach, ideological warfare, public diplomacy, strategic communication) and over whether the goal was to change the minds of all Muslims or only some, such as the already radicalised or the vulnerable young.

The result was confusion and the expenditure of millions of dollars with little evident benefit. Fundamental questions remained unanswered. How do you defeat an *idea*? Is it realistic for the United States—with over 400 military facilities in the Middle East and tens of thousands of troops fighting in two Muslim countries—to expect to win over a deeply sceptical Muslim public opinion?

* * *

'A conquering civilisation doesn't have terrorism,' the Muslim philosopher Seyyed Hossein Nasr has remarked. 'The conquered have terrorism.'[5]

What I have described as the 'Muslim revolt' is the product of a double failure: that of the régimes of the Muslim world to make a successful transition to modernity, and that of the West to deal intelligently and equitably with a part of the world vital to its strategic interests. From the 1970s on, movements set out under the banner of Islam to challenge the dominion of their own unjust governments and the hegemony of an unjust West. They found religion to be a powerful instrument of protest but a poor instrument of governance.

By the mid-1990s, the revolt of Islam had achieved impressive results at the grass roots but had, for the most part, failed to make the breakthrough to power. Politically, it was running out of steam.[6] As the Islamists kept up their challenge and the same old régimes clung stubbornly to power, there was a stalemate. This left the Islamists with few attractive options. Some—in Egypt, for example—retreated into civil society, deciding their best bet was to build up their strength over the long term through professional associations, welfare groups, human-rights organisations and websites devoted to Islam and Muslim causes. Others, as was later the case in Turkey, were ready to relinquish their Islamist ideology in order to win power, even if this required painful compromises with secularism and modernity.

A third option, taken by Al-Qaeda and the new jihadists, was to reject political gradualism and compromise and take the battle to the 'far enemy'—the United States and the West.[7] This idea was radically new and, even among jihadists, highly controversial. Bin Laden and his colleagues adopted this strategy partly out of choice, partly from necessity. Having themselves emerged from the Muslim Brotherhood (or at least its Qutbist wing), they argued that the Brotherhood's strategy had failed and must be abandoned. In their eyes, the future lay not in Islamo-nationalism—implanting Islamism in one country—but in an Islamist internationalism committed to a new kind of global revolutionary struggle. This option seemed the more plausible because many of the jihadists had, in any case, been displaced from their countries of origin by government repression. So, they argued, if the struggle could no longer be waged with any hope of success against the 'near enemy'—in, say, Egypt or Algeria or (in Bin Laden's case) Saudi Arabia—it must be waged in a new way from the fringes of the Muslim *umma*—from Afghanistan in the east and from Europe and America in the west. The periphery was attractive not because the Middle East no longer mattered but because it offered sanctuary.

From this sprang the logic of 9/11. Bin Laden and his Egyptian deputy Ayman al-Zawahiri 'knew that no operation they could mount in the United States or Europe would be capable of robbing the West of its power ... Consequently, the real purpose in striking the far enemy at home was not just to create mass casualties but also to provoke the United States to strike back and invade Muslim lands'.[8] The aim was to drag America into unwinnable regional conflicts, just as the Soviet Union had been sucked into an unwinnable war in Afghanistan in the 1980s. At the time, when the defeat and collapse of the Soviet superpower were still fresh in Muslim minds, the notion of attacking the American giant did not appear so very foolish. With Bin Laden's charisma and money and Zawahiri's strategic planning, Al-Qaeda attracted both attention and support as a new force willing and able to take on the West.

* * *

Why does the global *jihad* have such appeal among the world's disaffected Muslims? In large part because winning Muslim hearts and minds, far from being tangential to Al-Qaeda's purpose, has always been central to it—and the movement has addressed the task with skill and resourcefulness. David Kilcullen, in his book *The Accidental Guerrilla*, describes Al-Qaeda's prime function as being that of 'a propaganda and incitement hub'. 'The information side of [Al-Qaeda's] operation is primary; the physical is merely the tool to achieve a propaganda result.'[9]

Central to the jihadist strategy is a powerful narrative with three interlocking elements. It is first and foremost a narrative of humiliation, and one painted in primary colours. The core of the narrative is that the West—armed with traditional forms of military and economic power and with the newer instruments of globalisation—is at war with Islam. Daily, hour-by-hour evidence of the West's aggressive designs comes from conflict zones (Palestine, Iraq, Afghanistan, Chechnya, Kashmir) in which Muslims are victims or are seen as victims. Reinforcing the message from real wars is the message from 'culture wars'—such as the headscarf controversy and the cartoon affair—which are taken as further proof of the West's implacable hostility.

All these conflicts and controversies, big and small, act like tributaries feeding into a single river. Their cumulative message, repeated time and again, is of the humiliation of Muslims by a Western world which is at worst complicit in attacking

191

and belittling Muslims and at best cynically indifferent to Muslim suffering. If this narrative were entirely without substance its appeal might be less potent and it might be easier to counter. But it has enough substance to be credible and this gives jihadist propaganda plenty of scope for the orchestration of grievance.

Second, the jihadists proffer a seductive remedy for Muslim humiliation: redemptive violence. This is the flip-side of humiliation. Violence, legitimised by religion, wipes away the stain of humiliation and defeat: it 'de-humiliates'.[10] It transforms shame into pride and powerlessness into power. Regardless of its consequences, it is a kind of victory and hence an end in itself.

Third, this narrative of humiliation and de-humiliation is conveyed—effectively, instantaneously, globally—through intensely powerful imagery. Think for a moment of the attack on the Twin Towers. Whatever else it was, 9/11 was an extraordinary televisual moment. Al-Qaeda had not shot the footage, but the effect was as if it had; and it has adopted those graphic images as its trademark. A second example, and one which had an electrifying impact on jihadists and their target audience, was the beheading, on video, of the American hostage Nick Berg in Iraq in May 2004. That brutal moment, with Berg in his orange jumpsuit, crossed a new threshold in internet violence. It also catapulted the leader of Al-Qaeda in Iraq, Abu Musab al-Zarqawi, into the forefront of the global movement. The internet transformed Zarqawi from a small-time thug into a star performer of the *jihad*.[11]

The use of the internet by radical Islamists, for operational as well as propaganda purposes, is well documented.[12] In its mastery of the most modern means of communication, Al-Qaeda is a child of globalisation. Globalisation made it possible. Some of its operations, including the 9/11 attacks, were conceived in one continent, planned in another and carried out in a third. After 9/11, with the loss of its Afghan base, it could scarcely have stayed in business if it had not 'regrouped in cyberspace'.[13]

These three elements taken together—the narrative of humiliation, the legitimising role of violence and the power of globalised imagery—are a potent mix, which helps explain why the jihadist message has such wide appeal, well beyond the relatively small circle of radical activists. The Al-Qaeda narrative gives young Muslims identity, ideology and instrument: it tells them who they are, why they should act and what they should do. Even if Al-Qaeda the organisation has been weakened as a result of the US-led counter-attack since 9/11, Al-Qaeda the idea remains strong, and the idea will outlast it.

In the race to win hearts and minds, the West has struggled to catch up. The Bush administration left a toxic legacy whose effects will be felt for some time to come. Its framing, as well as its conduct, of the battle against the global *jihad* has hobbled the efforts of its successors. By designating the struggle a 'war on terror', Bush over-emphasised its military (as opposed to ideological) character and inflated Al-Qaeda into a global menace of grotesque proportions. This error was compounded by a tendency to lump all Islamist movements together—the Sunni with the Shi'a, the Islamo-nationalists with the internationalists—into some vast, amorphous 'axis of evil'. The enemy became terror writ large, rather than a specific group with its own history, aims and limitations.

At the same time, invading Afghanistan in 2001 and Iraq in 2003 played into Al-Qaeda's hands by appearing to validate its narrative of Western aggression and Muslim humiliation. This narrative was reinforced by the photographs of abuse at the Abu Ghraib prison in Baghdad and by the illegality of Guantanamo.

The in-coming Obama administration's ideas of how to redefine the global struggle against extremism were set out in August 2009, in a speech by the president's senior adviser on counter-terrorism, John Brennan.[14] Brennan, a former CIA analyst, set out five elements of the new approach. First, the fight against violent extremism was being 'returned to its proper place'. To view the world through the 'narrow prism of terrorism' was to allow Al-Qaeda to set the agenda and to 'foment a clash of civilisations in which the United States and Islam are seen as distinct identities that are in conflict'.

Second, important bits of the old terminology had to be discarded. The new administration no longer referred to the 'war on terrorism' (which confused ends and means). It had dropped the terms 'global war', 'jihad' and 'jihadist' (which it believed risked reinforcing Al-Qaeda's own self-image). It even shunned, though Brennan did not say so, the term 'Muslim world': the president now spoke, as he did in his Cairo speech, of 'Muslims around the world'.

Third, there must be a 'broader, more accurate understanding of the causes and conditions that help fuel violent extremism'. Poverty and lack of education did not cause terrorism, but they made people 'more susceptible to ideologies of violence and death'. Such problems therefore had to be dealt with. Fourth, addressing these 'upstream' factors, as Brennan called them, was 'ultimately not a military operation but a political, economic and social campaign to meet the basic needs and legitimate grievances of ordinary people'. Finally, the new approach required integrating 'every element of American power' in order to discourage violent extremism. The approach had to be multi–national as well as multi–dimensional. That meant, in places such as Afghanistan, Pakistan and Iraq, training armies, encouraging the democratic process, working with governments to bring about development and end corruption, and harnessing 'our greatest asset of all—the power of America's moral example'.

Much of this was scarcely new. But it had a new tone. It emanated from an administration with friendlier and less muscular body language, and one that was committed to disengage from Iraq, even if it was reinforcing its presence in Afghanistan.

* * *

Experts from Europe and the United States had gathered in Stockholm to discuss counter-terrorism and the newly-fashionable concept of counter-insurgency. There were senior soldiers and policemen, intelligence people, diplomats, think-tank experts, a few journalists and a bevy of company executives selling the latest security gizmos. The mood was sombre. The military men were grappling with the novel idea that the battle was no longer only on the ground but in the mind. Force had to be calibrated accordingly. Not everyone was comfortable with this new emphasis on winning hearts and minds.[15]

One of the keynote speakers at the conference was a leading American guru of counter-insurgency, Lieutenant-Colonel John Nagl. Nagl, in his early forties, represents a new breed of soldier-scholar. After graduating from West Point he commanded a tank platoon in the Gulf war of 1991 and then went to Oxford, where he gained a PhD with a thesis on the neglected subject of counter-insurgency. In 2002 his Oxford dissertation on the counter-insurgency lessons of Malaya and Vietnam was published as a book called *Learning to Eat Soup with a Knife* (a title derived from T. E. Lawrence's observation in *Seven Pillars of Wisdom* that fighting an insurgency is 'messy and slow, like eating soup with a knife'). Nagl returned to West Point as a professor, taking time off to serve with an army battalion in Anbar province in Iraq.[16]

Nagl and his Australian colleague David Kilcullen are practitioners as well as theoreticians of the new warfare. They dislike the term 'war on terror' and prefer to speak of the 'long war', which they characterise as a global counter-insurgency. The critical difference between a terrorist and an insurgent is that an insurgent enjoys a greater degree of local support. Indiscriminate use of force only strengthens that base of support. As Nagl puts it, 'It's at the grass-roots level that you're trying to win. You can kill enemy soldiers—that's not the only issue. You also need to dry up their support. You can't just use the military. It's got to be a constant din of propaganda; it's got to be economic support; it's got to be elections. As long as you only go after the guy with the weapon, you're missing the most important part.'[17]

Nagl and Kilcullen are careful to add that the term 'global counter-insurgency' should not be taken to imply that Gaza, Kashmir, Chechnya, Iraq, Afghanistan and the rest are all part of one big fight. Insurgencies must be narrowly defined: they are rooted in local grievances and acquire local dynamics, even if there are linkages with groups elsewhere. The watchword is 'disaggregate'.[18]

A key conclusion from all this is that information is essential to winning hearts and minds—something Al-Qaeda has understood and practised more successfully than its adversaries. According to classical counter-insurgency doctrine, only twenty-five per cent of the task is military and seventy-five per cent non-military. That imposes immense challenges on a large, cumbersome bureaucracy like that of the United States. It requires the formulation of an overall strategy which is both understood and implemented by all the relevant branches of government—politicians, diplomats, spies and development agencies, no less than the different arms of the military.

The consensus among the experts at the conference was that no such overarching strategy existed. When I asked John Nagl how long the 'long war' would last, he replied, 'Thirty years if we get it right; a hundred years if we get it wrong.'

* * *

Ever since 9/11, there has been intense debate about how young Muslims are radicalised. The average age of the 9/11 hijackers was twenty-five; that of the London bombers twenty-two; when Bouyeri killed Van Gogh in Amsterdam he was twenty-six. In his book *Leaderless Jihad*, Marc Sageman analyses radicalisation in the Muslim diaspora—viewed by the jihadists as an important new pool of potential recruits—and suggests it has four main elements (though they do not necessarily occur in a neat chronological sequence).

First, there is a catalyst: an incident involving the suffering of a fellow Muslim in, say, Gaza which provokes a sense of moral outrage. Second, this incident—this act of moral violation—is given a context: it is viewed as part of a global war against Islam. (Sageman calls this a 'morality play'.) Third, the scene in Gaza resonates with the individual's personal experience of, say, racism or unemployment living in the West: the local fuses with the global. And finally the individual is recruited into a network. This becomes a surrogate family which takes over his life and eventually grooms him to take part in an operation. Many Muslims have the first three experiences; far fewer take the final step.[19]

Sageman's paradigm is persuasive because it fits the available evidence. The different factors that experts have put forward—the role of regional conflicts and of Western policy towards them, the crisis of identity experienced by many young Muslims living in the West, the power of jihadist ideology and its accompanying narrative, the 'buddy' principle, which leads Sageman to argue that radicalisation is a social rather than an individual experience—become mutually reinforcing rather than mutually exclusive. The jihadist narrative would not be effective without the foreign-policy component which is its core. The individual would not be so susceptible to that narrative had he not himself experienced some form of Western hostility or rejection. None of these things would be decisive if there were not well-organised networks capable of recruiting vulnerable individuals.

Whether these networks in the West are home-grown, and thus part of a 'leaderless *jihad*', has been hotly debated. Bruce Hoffman argues that Al-Qaeda Central has revived itself in the remote and lawless Afghan-Pakistani border region and has played a role in many of the recent plots in the West—successful or unsuccessful—which have been described, in his view misleadingly, as home-grown.[20] More evidence may emerge of what powers of command-and-control Al-Qaeda Central still has, beyond its immediate south Asian area of operation. In the meantime, two phenomena coexist: the original Al-Qaeda leadership, now dwindling in number but still a potent force in the Afghanistan-Pakistan-India region—arguably the central and most dangerous front in the global *jihad*—and the larger and much more diffuse and decentralised phenomenon which Sageman calls the 'Al-Qaeda social movement'. The relationship between the two is not crystal-clear, but they represent two sets of distinct, if overlapping, challenges.

* * *

A cartoon by Plantu on the front page of *Le Monde* shows a group of policemen looking at two mug-shots. The first is of a man with a round face, a curly beard and a Muslim prayer-cap. The second is of a man with a round face, a curly beard and a Muslim prayer-cap. In fact the two pictures are identical. Beneath one is written—in French—'Good Muslim' and beneath the other 'Bad Muslim'.[21]

For the policeman in Paris or New York, just as for the soldier in Iraq or Afghanistan, one of the essential tasks is to drive a wedge between the radical Islamists and the Muslim communities in which they live and seek to draw support. This is easier said than done. The notion that one can readily identify 'moderates' and 'radicals', and then set about strengthening the one and marginalising the other, is appealing but simplistic. It reduces a wide spectrum of opinion to two crude categories, and begs the question of what constitutes moderation. (Is a moderate simply someone who does what we want?) The issue of Muslim opinion needs to be treated with rather more care. Although opinion polls have their drawbacks—why would someone in a closed society such as Saudi Arabia reveal their innermost thoughts to a stranger?—they can provide pointers. Two leading polling organisations, Pew and Gallup, have attempted to survey Muslim opinion in a systematic fashion; for example in a Gallup poll in 2007 which was the largest of its kind and formed the basis for a book called *Who Speaks for Islam?*[22]

Among the points it highlighted was, first, the depth of Muslim hostility to American foreign policy. Well before the arrival of George Bush in the White House, Muslims considered that America was unduly biased towards Israel, acted in an aggressive manner in the Middle East and displayed a lack of respect for Islam. That view intensified significantly during the Bush presidency. Second, most of the Muslims polled said they favoured democracy, a finding which called into question Bush's view that radical Muslims 'hate our freedoms'. Third, Muslim grievances are not the preserve of the radical few but are to a considerable extent shared within the mainstream. This underlines how unhelpful it is to try to make facile distinctions between 'good Muslims' and 'bad Muslims'.

Imagine Muslim opinion as two circles. The large inner circle represents the majority; the small outer rim the violent *jihadi* fringe. What both have in common—the core of the circle—is a shared set of grievances, both local and global, against the West and against the governments of the Muslim world. There is a common conviction that the US-led West is powerful and the Muslim *umma* weak; that the West is either hostile to the Muslims of Palestine, Iraq, Chechnya and other conflict zones or coldly indifferent to their fate; that Muslim governments are corrupt, autocratic and in most cases subservient to the West; and that Muslims have the right to resist occupation by non-Muslim powers.

Seen in this light, the mainstream is not moderate; it is angry. But while there is significant common ground between the mainstream and the radical fringe, there are also significant differences. The mainstream wants to see the *umma* grow stronger *vis-à-vis* the West, but does not share the radical *jihadi* view of history as an unending conflict between believers and infidels. The majority are critical of the West for what it does; the minority hate it for what it is. The majority resent the West's perceived hypocrisy over democracy; the minority reject democracy. The majority feel revulsion at the killing of civilians; the minority are ready to justify the killing of civilians, even Muslim civilians.

This is a sketch of Muslim opinion, not a map. But it provides an alternative to the futile hunt for 'good guys' and 'bad guys' and instead requires us to look more closely at the nature of Muslim grievances and, in particular, the vexed question of Western foreign policy. The former British Prime Minister Tony Blair described Muslim indignation over Western policy as 'a wholly imagined grievance'.[23] But if such grievances are imaginary—are essentially manufactured—it is hard to see why the narrative of humiliation should have such force. Al-Qaeda and others are, to be sure, highly skilful in amplifying and orchestrating grievance. Bin Laden is able to frame the conflict as a global battle between good and evil, between truth and falsehood. But manipulation of grievance does not necessarily invalidate it.

Across the heartlands of Islam, from Mauritania to Mindanao, Muslims are for the most part badly governed, their human rights abused, their economic development stunted. These problems are real, and they cannot all be laid directly at the door of the West. But to ignore or downplay the role of outside powers—their feckless interventions, their indulgence of autocratic rulers, their double-talk on human rights and democracy—is to close our eyes to an important part of the problem.

'We feed terrorism,' observed Douglas Hurd, a former British Foreign Secretary, 'by killing a lot of people, whether in Gaza or in Fallujah or in Chechnya.' By their conduct in these places, the Israelis, the Americans and the Russians are 'manufacturing terrorists all the time'.[24] In other words, prolonged occupation perpetuates deeply-rooted grievances and ensures a constant flow of fresh recruits for the local struggle and, all too often, for the global *jihad* as well. Shutting down these 'factories of terrorism' would do more to win Muslim hearts and minds than multi-million-dollar advertising campaigns, ill-conceived efforts to export democracy and simplistic notions of 'good Muslims' and 'bad Muslims'.

Few of these regional conflicts, and others around the world in which Muslims are involved, are readily amenable to solution. But the most important of them—the Israeli–Palestinian problem—deserves focused and sustained attention. Bruce Riedel, challenging the view that the issue is tangential to the *jihad* or that Bin Laden only picked it up belatedly and opportunistically, calls it 'the central all-consuming issue for al Qaeda'.[25] One expert has even described the belief that Palestine is irrelevant to the 'war on terror' as 'arguably the greatest delusion of the post-9/11 era'.[26]

The triple challenge, then, is to understand Islam, Islamism and jihadism in all their diversity; to appreciate the roots of Muslim grievance; and, on this basis, to craft a set of co-ordinated policies—local, regional and global—designed to foster a less hostile and more equitable relationship between the West and Islam.

A tall order? As tall as the Twin Towers. But without a new approach, based on a surer grasp of Islamism and its discontents, the Muslim revolt will continue for generations to come.

NOTES

INTRODUCTION

1. Robert Leiken, 'Europe's Angry Muslims', *Foreign Affairs*, July/August 2005, p. 122.
2. See Graham E. Fuller and Ian O. Lesser, *A Sense of Siege: The Geopolitics of Islam and the West*, Boulder, Colorado: Westview, 1995.
3. The top ten Muslim populations are:

Indonesia	203 million	88%
Pakistan	174 million	96%
India	160 million	13.4%
Bangladesh	145 million	83%
Egypt	78.5 million	94%
Nigeria	78 million	50%
Iran	74 million	99%
Turkey	73 million	98%
Morocco	34 million	98%
Algeria	32 million	99%

(The figures show the number of Muslims and their percentage within the overall population of each country; *Mapping the Global Muslim Population*, Washington, DC: Pew Research Center, October 2009; www.pewforum.org)
4. Albert Hourani, *Europe and the Middle East*, London: Macmillan, 1980, p. 15. He is paraphrasing Clifford Geertz's book *Islam Observed*, but there can be little doubt that the sentiments are his own.
5. Ali A. Allawi, *The Crisis of Islamic Civilization*, New Haven and London: Yale University Press, 2009.

CHAPTER 1: DREAM OF REVIVAL

1. Ibn Battuta, *Travels in Asia and Africa 1325–1354*, London: Routledge, 1929; paperback edition, 1983, p. 50. In this chapter I have drawn on two BBC World Service radio series, *Waiting for the Dawn: Muslims in the Modern World* (2002) and *Islam: Faith and Power* (1995).

2. Interview with Hasan Hanafi, Cairo, March 2002. For profiles of Hanafi, see John L. Esposito and John O. Voll, *Makers of Contemporary Islam*, New York and Oxford: Oxford University Press, 2001; and Caryle Murphy, *Passion for Islam: Shaping the Modern Middle East: The Egyptian Experience*, New York: Scribner, 2002.

3. Murphy, *Passion for Islam*, p. 224.

4. Ira Lapidus, *A History of Islamic Societies*, Cambridge: Cambridge University Press, 2nd edition, 2002, p. xx. For the period of expansion, see Hugh Kennedy, *The Great Arab Conquests*, London: Weidenfeld & Nicolson, 2007.

5. See Michael Cook, *Forbidding Wrong in Islam*, Cambridge: Cambridge University Press, 2003; a shorter version of a much larger study, *Commanding Right and Forbidding Wrong in Islamic Thought*, published two years earlier.

6. Albert Hourani, *Islam in European Thought*, Cambridge: Cambridge University Press, 1991, p. 7.

7. R. W. Southern, *Western Views of Islam in the Middle Ages*, Cambridge, Mass.: Harvard University Press, 1962, pp. 3–5.

8. Thomas Asbridge, *The First Crusade*, London: Simon and Schuster, 2004; paperback edition, 2005, p. 2. On the 'imagined history' of the Crusades, see Christopher Tyerman, *Fighting for Christendom: Holy War and the Crusades*, Oxford and New York: Oxford University Press, 2004.

9. Malise Ruthven, *A Satanic Affair: Salman Rushdie and the Wrath of Islam*, London: Hogarth Press, revised edition, 1991, p. 154. 'The assumption of dominance,' he writes, 'proceeds from a theology of power which rests uneasily in psyches facing the reality of powerlessness.'

10. Quotations from Al-Jabarti are from Albert Hourani, *Arabic Thought in the Liberal Age, 1798–1939*, Oxford and New York:

Oxford University Press, 1962; paperback edition, 1970, p. 51; and Hourani, *Islam in European Thought*, p. 15.

11. Albert Hourani, reviewing Edward Said's *Orientalism* in the *New York Review of Books*, 8 March 1979.

12. Max Rodenbeck, *Cairo: The City Victorious*, New York: Knopf, 1999, pp. 121–3. For a fuller account of the French occupation, see Juan Cole, *Napoleon's Egypt: Invading the Middle East*, New York: Palgrave Macmillan, 2007.

13. Hourani, *Arabic Thought*, p. 141.

14. Quoted in Yvonne Haddad, 'Muhammad Abduh: Pioneer of Islamic Reform' in Ali Rahnema (ed.), *Pioneers of Islamic Revival*, London: Zed Books, 2nd edition, 2005, pp. 35–6.

15. Haddad, 'Muhammad Abduh', pp. 56–8.

16. L. Carl Brown, *Religion and State: The Muslim Approach to Politics*, New York: Columbia University Press, 2000, p. 140.

17. Hourani, *Arabic Thought*, p. 144.

18. Afaf Lutfi al-Sayyid Marsot, *A Short History of Modern Egypt*, Cambridge: Cambridge University Press, 1985, pp. 75.

19. Marsot, *A Short History*, pp. 75–6.

20. Interview with Mamoun Hudeibi, Cairo, April 1995.

21. Quoted in Brynjar Lia, *The Society of the Muslim Brothers in Egypt: The Rise of an Islamic Mass Movement 1928–1942*, Reading: Ithaca Press, 1998, p. 28. This is an invaluable account of the Brotherhood's formative period.

22. For details of Hanafi's intellectual development, see Esposito and Voll, *Makers of Contemporary Islam*, pp. 72–3.

23. Gilles Kepel, *Muslim Extremism in Egypt: The Prophet and Pharaoh*, Berkeley: University of California Press, 1985, pp. 43ff. Extracts from *Milestones* can be found in Albert J. Bergesen, *The Sayyid Qutb Reader*, New York and London: Routledge, 2008.

24. Bergesen, *The Sayyid Qutb Reader*, p. 35.

25. Quoted in Charles Tripp, 'Sayyid Qutb: The Political Vision' in Ali Rahnema (ed.), *Pioneers of Islamic Revival*, p. 171.

26. Wilfred Cantwell Smith, *Islam in Modern History*, Princeton: Princeton University Press, 1957, p. 41.

27. Interview with Mamoun Hudeibi, Cairo, April 1995. Hudeibi went on to become leader, or 'guide', of the Brotherhood in 2002.

When he died in 2004, at the age of eighty-three, he was one of the last survivors of the old guard.

28. Extract from 'Lament from the June Sun' by Abdul-Wahab al-Bayati, translated by Desmond Stewart, *Encounter*, October 1971. Originally written in 1968, the poem was hugely popular, reflecting the view that Arab leaders were self-serving and, for all their talk of Arab unity, badly divided among themselves.

29. From a series of articles by Maxime Rodinson in *Le Monde*, 6–8 December 1978. For an English translation, see Maxime Rodinson, 'Islam resurgent?' in his *Marxism and the Muslim World*, New York and London: Monthly Review Press, 1981.

30. The background and career of Zawahiri are described in Lawrence Wright, *The Looming Tower: Al-Qaeda and the Road to 9/11*, New York: Random House, 2006; and Bruce Riedel, *The Search for Al Qaeda: Its Leadership, Ideology and Future*, Washington, DC: Brookings Institution Press, 2008.

31. Interview with Muhammad Said al-Ashmawi, Cairo, March 2002. Excerpts from his book can be found in Charles Kurzman (ed.), *Liberal Islam: A Sourcebook*, New York and Oxford: Oxford University Press, 1998, pp. 49–56.

32. For the Abou-Zeid case, see Murphy, *Passion for Islam*, pp. 200–13.

33. Jennifer Noyon, *Islam, Politics and Pluralism*, London: Royal Institute of International Affairs, 2003, p. 6.

34. Interview with Heba Raouf Ezzat, Cairo, May 1995.

35. Hasan Hanafi, 'The Relevance of the Islamic Alternative in Egypt', *Arab Studies Quarterly*, Spring 1982.

CHAPTER 2: MARTYRS FOR HUSSEIN

1. Ashura processions, Tehran, June 1995. This chapter draws on visits to Iran in 1995, 1997 and 2002 and on two BBC World Service radio series, *Islam: Faith and Power* (1995) and *Waiting for the Dawn* (2002).

2. I have found the following books on the Shi'a helpful: Graham E. Fuller and Rend Rahim Francke, *The Arab Shi'a: The Forgotten Muslims*, London: Palgrave Macmillan, 2000; Yitzhak Nakhash, *Reaching for Power: The Shi'a in the Modern Arab World*, Prince-

ton: Princeton University Press, 2006; and, above all, Roy Mottahedeh, *The Mantle of the Prophet: Religion and Politics in Iran*, London: Chatto & Windus, 1985; Penguin, 1987; which not only illuminates modern Iranian history but in an uncanny way takes the reader inside the world of Shi'ite Islam. (Its original subtitle, 'Knowledge and Power in Iran', more accurately reflects its purpose.)

3. Gavin Young, *Iraq: Land of Two Rivers*, London: Collins, 1980, p. 126.

4. Mottahedeh, *The Mantle of the Prophet*, p. 34. References are to the paperback edition of 1987.

5. Brian Lapping, *End of Empire*, London: Grenada, 1985, p. 193. For a fuller account of the opening-up of Iran to the world economy, and of the course of the Constitutional Revolution, see Ervand Abrahamian, *A History of Modern Iran*, Cambridge: Cambridge University Press, 2008, pp. 36–41.

6. Mottahedeh, *The Mantle of the Prophet*, p. 53.

7. Lapping, *End of Empire*, p. 194.

8. Abrahamian, *A History of Modern Iran*, p. 67.

9. Mottahedeh, *The Mantle of the Prophet*, p. 125. A readable and well-researched account of the Mossadeq episode can be found in Lapping, *End of Empire*. For fuller and more recent accounts, see Abrahamian, *A History of Modern Iran*, and Stephen Kinzer, *All the Shah's Men*, New York: Wiley, 2003.

10. For an account of Khomeini's life and thought, see Baqer Moin, 'Khomeini's Search for Perfection: Theory and Reality' in Ali Rahnema (ed.), *Pioneers of Islamic Revival*, London: Zed Books, 2nd edition, 2005; and the same author's biography, *Khomeini: Life of the Ayatollah*, London: I. B. Tauris, 1999.

11. Quoted in Mottahedeh, *The Mantle of the Prophet*, pp. 245–6.

12. Interviews in Tehran, June 1995.

13. Christopher de Bellaigue, *In the Rose Garden of the Martyrs: A Memoir of Iran*, London: HarperCollins, 2004, p. 26.

14. De Bellaigue, *In the Rose Garden*, pp. 136–156. By the end of the war, he writes, 'Iranians no longer expected to hear the truth from their leaders.' The role of the war in the unravelling of the revolution is the central theme of this vivid and original book.

15. The killings, Ganji's exposure of them and his subsequent trial and imprisonment are brilliantly recounted by de Bellaigue, *In the Rose Garden*, pp. 233–51. Ganji's incarceration lasted from 2000 to 2006. For an example of his political writing, see 'The Latter-Day Sultan: Power and Politics in Iran', *Foreign Affairs*, November/ December 2008.

16. 'The Paradox of *Velayat-e-Faqih* and the Islamic Republic', an unpublished text by Mehdi Ha'eri–Yazdi. Ha'eri–Yazdi died in 1999 at the age of seventy-six.

17. Demographic data are from Keith Crane, Rollie Lal and Jeffrey Martini, *Iran's Political, Demographic, and Economic Challenges*, Santa Monica: Rand, 2008.

18. Interview with Shirin Ebadi, Tehran, June 1995.

19. Abrahamian, *A History of Modern Iran*, p. 188.

20. For a summary of Soroush's ideas, see Valla Vakili, 'Abdolkarim Soroush and Critical Discourse in Iran', in John L. Esposito and John O. Voll (eds.), *Makers of Contemporary Islam*, Oxford and New York: Oxford University Press, 2001. Some of Soroush's essays and speeches are brought together in Mahmoud Sadri and Ahmad Sadri (eds.), *Reason, Freedom, and Democracy in Islam: Essential Writings of Abdolkarim Soroush*, New York and Oxford: Oxford University Press, 2000.

21. Quoted in Yasuyuki Matsunaga, 'Mohsen Kadivar, an Advocate of Postrevivalist Islam in Iran', in Lloyd Ridgeon (ed.), *Iranian Intellectuals: 1997–2007*, London and New York: Routledge, 2008, p. 58.

22. Interview with Kadivar, Tehran, May 2002.

23. The core values are those identified in Karim Sadjadpour, *Reading Khamenei: The World View of Iran's Most Powerful Leader*, Washington, DC: Carnegie Endowment for International Peace, 2008; www.ceip.org. One might add another core value: empowerment. In seeking to replace the cadres of the *ancien régime*, the mullahs have enfranchised new social groups including, albeit under the chador, women from outside the traditional élite.

24. See, for example, Chris Kraul and Sebastian Rotella, 'Hezbollah Presence in Venezuela Feared', *Los Angeles Times*, 27 August 2008.

25. An incident treated more fully in the chapter on Saudi Arabia, below.
26. See John L. Esposito (ed.), *The Iranian Revolution: Its Global Impact*, Miami: Florida International University Press, 1990, which assesses the revolution's influence in the Middle East, Africa and Asia, a decade on. For a valuable collection of essays on the period between 1979 and 2009, see *The Iranian Revolution at 30*, an on-line publication of the Middle East Institute, Washington, DC, 2009; www.mideasti.org.

CHAPTER 3: CULTURE OF *JIHAD*

1. Interview with Hamid Gul, Rawalpindi, April 2002. This chapter draws on two BBC World Service radio series: *Islam: Faith and Power* (1995) and *Waiting for the Dawn* (2002).
2. Quoted in Husain Haqqani, *Pakistan: Between Mosque and Military*, Washington, DC: Carnegie Endowment for International Peace, 2005, p. 12. The speech was delivered on 11 August 1947. Official versions were subsequently edited to remove its clear secularist thrust.
3. Robert G. Wirsing, 'Political Islam, Pakistan, and the Geopolitics of Religious Identity', in Yoichiro Sato (ed.), *Growth and Governance in Asia*, Honolulu: Asia-Pacific Center for Security Studies, 2004, p. 175.
4. 'The Coup in Pakistan', *Newsweek*, 18 July 1977.
5. Stephen Philip Cohen, *The Idea of Pakistan*, Washington, DC: Brookings Institution Press, 2004, pp. 169–70.
6. Mumtaz Ahmad, 'The Crescent and the Sword: Islam, the Military, and Political Legitimacy in Pakistan', *Middle East Journal*, Summer 1996.
7. Aziz Ahmad, 'India', in Joseph Schacht and C. E. Bosworth (eds.), *The Legacy of Islam*, New York and Oxford: Oxford University Press, 1974, pp. 134ff. For a fuller account of the Great Mughals, see Francis Robinson, *The Mughal Emperors*, London: Thames & Hudson, 2007.
8. Aziz Ahmad, 'India', pp. 137ff.
9. Interview with Suroosh Irfani, Lahore, April 2002.

10. Emmanuel Sivan, *Radical Islam*, New Haven and London: Yale University Press, 2nd edition, 1990, p. 39.

11. Interview with Anis Ahmad, Islamabad, May 1995.

12. Seyyed Vali Reza Nasr, 'Mawdudi and the Jama'at-i Islami' in Ali Rahnema (ed.), *Pioneers of Islamic Revival*, London: Zed Books, 2nd edition, 2005, pp. 105–6.

13. Nasr, 'Mawdudi', pp. 118–9.

14. Don Belt, 'Struggle for the Soul of Pakistan', *National Geographic*, September 2007, p. 45.

15. On the debate surrounding the numbers of *madrasas* (both registered and unregistered) and how many students they have, see Wirsing, 'Political Islam, Pakistan and the Geopolitics of Religious Identity', p. 172; Belt, 'Struggle for the Soul of Pakistan', p. 44; and Muhammad Qasim Zaman (see note 16, below).

16. Muhammad Qasim Zaman, 'Tradition and Authority in Deobandi Madrasas of South Asia', in Robert W. Hefner and Muhammad Qasim Zaman (eds.), *Schooling Islam: The Culture and Politics of Modern Muslim Education*, Princeton: Princeton University Press, 2007, pp. 71–4.

17. On the role of the ISI in the Afghan war, see Shuja Nawaz, *Crossed Swords: Pakistan, Its Army, and the Wars Within*, New York and Oxford: Oxford University Press, 2008, pp. 373ff.

18. Interview with Bruce Riedel, Washington, DC, October 2008.

19. For the figure of $6 billion—distinctly higher than earlier estimates—see Bruce Riedel, *The Search for Al Qaeda*, Washington, DC: Brookings Institution Press, 2008, p. 62. Prince Turki's remark is quoted in Steve Coll, *Ghost Wars*, New York: Penguin, 2005, p. 72.

20. Stephen Engelberg, 'One Man and a Global Web of Violence', *New York Times*, 14 January 2001.

21. Engelberg, 'One Man and a Global Web'; Lawrence Wright, *The Looming Tower: Al-Qaeda and the Road to 9/11*, London: Allen Lane, 2006, pp. 131–44. For an account of the life, work and influence of Abdullah Azzam, see Thomas Hegghammer's profile of him in Gilles Kepel and Jean-Pierre Milelli (eds.), *Al Qaeda in Its Own Words*, Cambridge, Mass.: Harvard University Press, 2008, pp. 81–101.

22. Interview with Steve Coll, Washington, DC, October 2008; and see *Ghost Wars*, pp. 164, 175–6.
23. Interview with Abdullah Anas, London, April 2001.
24. Interview with Bruce Riedel, Washington, DC, October 2008. He writes: 'The world quickly lost interest [in Afghanistan], including the United States. I served on George H. W. Bush's National Security Council in 1991 and 1992 and cannot recall a single senior-level meeting on the subject;' Riedel, *The Search for Al Qaeda*, p. 46.
25. Interviews in Lahore, April 2002.
26. Asma Jahangir, 'What the Protection of Women Act Does and What is Left Undone', Human Rights Commission of Pakistan, *State of Human Rights in 2006*, Lahore: 2007.
27. Interview with Suroush Irfani, Lahore, April 2002.
28. Interview with Hamid Gul, Rawalpindi, April 2002.
29. Hamid Gul, interview with Arnaud de Borchgrave, United Press International, 26 September 2001.
30. Zahid Hussain, *Frontline Pakistan: The Struggle with Militant Islam*, New York: Columbia University Press, 2007, pp. 81–2.
31. Coll, *Ghost Wars*, p. 479.
32. Nawaz, *Crossed Swords*, pp. 585 and 359.

CHAPTER 4: A BRIDGE TO AFRICA

1. Visit to Khartoum, March-April 1995. This chapter draws on material from the BBC World Service radio series *Islam: Faith and Power* (1995).
2. Interviews in Khartoum and London, March-April 1995.
3. Helen Metz (ed.), *Sudan: A Country Study*, Washington, DC: Library of Congress, 1991. On Sudan's role in the slave trade, see Ronald Segal, *Islam's Black Slaves: A History of Africa's Other Black Diaspora*, London: Atlantic Books, 2002.
4. Carolyn Fluehr-Lobban, 'Sudan' in John L. Esposito (ed.), *The Oxford Encyclopedia of the Modern Islamic World*, New York and Oxford: Oxford University Press, 1995, p. 99.
5. Brian Lapping, *End of Empire*, London: Granada, 1985; paperback edition, 1989, p. 287.

6. Peter Woodward, *US Policy and the Horn of Africa*, Farnham, Surrey: Ashgate, 2006, p. 40. I have relied on Woodward's chapter on Sudan, which provides an incisive account of the Islamist régime and its policies.

7. Raymond Bonner, 'Letter from Sudan', *New Yorker*, 13 July 1992.

8. Benjamin Stora, *Algeria, 1830–2000: A Short History*, Ithaca: Cornell University Press, 2001, p. 111.

9. Martin Evans and John Phillips, *Algeria: Anger of the Dispossessed*, New Haven and London: Yale University Press, 2007, p. 105.

10. Evans and Phillips, *Algeria*, p. 120.

11. William B. Quandt, *Between Ballots and Bullets: Algeria's Transition from Authoritarianism*, Washington, DC: Brookings Institution Press, 1998, p. 60.

12. Woodward, *US Policy and the Horn of Africa*, p. 47.

13. John L. Esposito and John O. Voll, *Makers of Contemporary Islam*, New York and Oxford: Oxford University Press, 2001, pp. 68–90, which I have drawn on for details of Turabi's life.

14. Woodward, *US Policy and the Horn of Africa*, p. 38.

CHAPTER 5: THE PIOUS ANCESTORS

1. The demonstration was on 14 October 2003. See 'Anger on Saudi Arabia's Streets', BBC News Online, 1 November 2003. This chapter draws on a series of visits to the kingdom between 1994 and 2007, and on the BBC World Service radio series *Jihad and the Petrodollar* (2007).

2. Visit to Dir'iyah, October 2007.

3. Wilfred Cantwell Smith, *Islam in Modern History*, Princeton: Princeton University Press, 1957, p. 42.

4. Interview with Prince Turki, Prague, October 2007.

5. Bernard Haykel, 'On the Nature of Salafi Thought and Action' in Roel Meijer (ed.), *Global Salafism: Islam's New Religious Movement*, London: Hurst, 2009. I am grateful to Professor Haykel for making this essay available to me ahead of publication.

6. The others were Muhammad Abduh, Mustafa Kemal Atatürk, Chaim Weizmann, Sultan Muhammad V of Morocco and Gamal

Abdel-Nasser. See Elizabeth Monroe's chapter on the Middle East in Alan Bullock (ed.), *The Twentieth Century*, London: Thames & Hudson, 1971.

7. Interviews in London, in 1990, for the BBC World Service radio series *The Making of the Middle East*.

8. Visit to WAMY, Riyadh, October 2007.

9. James P. Piscatori, 'Islamic Values and National Interest: The Foreign Policy of Saudi Arabia' in Adeed Dawisha (ed.), *Islam in Foreign Policy*, Cambridge: Cambridge University Press, 1983.

10. On the seizure of the mosque, see Yaroslav Trofimov, *The Siege of Mecca*, New York: Anchor Books, 2007. On the currents of Saudi opposition, see Mamoun Fandy, *Saudi Arabia: The Politics of Dissent*, London: Palgrave Macmillan, 1999.

11. The account of Bin Laden's youth is drawn from an interview with Khaled Batarfi, a newspaper editor in Jeddah, October 2003, and from Steve Coll, *The Bin Ladens*, London and New York: Penguin Press, 2008.

12. On the Sahwa, see Madawi Al-Rasheed, *Contesting the Saudi State: Islamic Voices from a New Generation*, Cambridge: Cambridge University Press, 2007.

13. Quoted in Joshua Teitelbaum, *Holier Than Thou: Saudi Arabia's Islamic Opposition*, Washington, DC: Washington Institute for Near East Policy, 2000, p. 29.

14. I have written in more detail about the petitions and Fahd's reforms in *Arabia after the Storm: Internal Stability of the Gulf Arab States*, London: Chatham House, 1992.

15. 'The Cracks in the Kingdom', *Economist*, 18 March 1995.

16. David B. Ottaway, *The King's Messenger: Prince Bandar Bin Sultan and America's Tangled Relationship with Saudi Arabia*, New York: Walker Books, 2008, p. 104.

17. See Toby Craig Jones, 'Rebellion on the Saudi Periphery: Modernity, Marginalization, and the Shi'a Uprising of 1979', *International Journal of Middle East Studies*, Vol. 38, No. 2, 2006.

18. The deal received little publicity at the time. For a summary, see Teitelbaum, *Holier Than Thou*, pp. 108–10. For a reconstruction of how the deal was struck, see Robert Lacey, *Inside the Kingdom*, New York: Viking, 2009, pp. 170–73. For background on the Saudi Shi'a, see Graham E. Fuller and Rend Rahim Francke,

The Arab Shi'a: The Forgotten Muslims, London: Palgrave Macmillan, 2000.

19. Bruce Riedel, *The Search for Al Qaeda: Its Leadership, Ideology, and Future*, Washington, DC: Brookings Institution Press, 2008, p. 51. See also Thomas Hegghammer, 'Deconstructing the Myth about al-Qa'ida and Khobar', *CTC Sentinel*, February 2008.

20. Bruce Riedel, 'Al-Qaeda Strikes Back', *Foreign Affairs*, May/June 2007.

21. On the crisis in US-Saudi relations, see my essay 'Ambivalent Ally: Saudi Arabia and the "War on Terror",' in Madawi Al-Rasheed (ed.), *Kingdom without Borders: Saudi Arabia's Political, Religious and Media Frontiers*, London: Hurst, 2008; and Rachel Bronson, *Thicker Than Oil: America's Uneasy Partnership with Saudi Arabia*, New York and Oxford: Oxford University Press, 2006.

22. Thomas Hegghammer, 'Islamist Violence and Régime Stability in Saudi Arabia', *International Affairs*, April 2008, pp. 709–10.

23. Bernard Haykel, 'On the Nature of Salafi Thought' (see note 5, above).

24. Christopher Boucek, *Saudi Arabia's 'Soft' Counterterrorism Strategy: Prevention, Rehabilitation, and Aftercare*, Washington, DC: Carnegie Endowment for International Peace, September 2008. The success of the rehabilitation programme has been the subject of debate.

25. Interview with Hassan al-Maliki, Riyadh, October 2007. See 'Jihad and the Saudi Petrodollar', BBC News Online, 15 November 2007.

26. Interview with Sam Roe, Chicago, September 2007. For a detailed investigation into the Benevolence case, see Sam Roe, Laurie Cohen and Stephen Franklin, 'How Saudi Wealth Fuelled Holy War', *Chicago Tribune*, 22 February 2004.

27. Interviews with Suliman al-Buthi in Riyadh, and with Dennis Lormel in Washington, DC, October 2007. Full accounts of the investigation of the two charities (Benevolence and Al-Haramain) can be found in National Commission on Terrorist Attacks upon the United States, *Monograph on Terrorist Financing*, Washington, DC: 9/11 Commission, 2004; www.9–11commission.gov. For a balanced account of Saudi charities and the debate sur-

rounding them, see Jon B. Alterman, 'Saudi Charities and Support for Terror', in Jon B. Alterman and Karin von Hippel (eds.), *Understanding Islamic Charities*, Washington, DC: Center for Strategic and International Studies, 2007.

28. National Commission on Terrorist Attacks upon the United States, *The 9/11 Commission Report*, New York: W. W. Norton, 2004, p. 171.

CHAPTER 6: THE TURKISH EXCEPTION

1. Interviews in Istanbul, April 2004. This chapter also draws on the BBC World Service radio series *Waiting for the Dawn* (2002).

2. Halide Edib, *The Turkish Ordeal*, New York and London: The Century Company, 1928, p. 185.

3. Quoted in Stephen Kinzer, *Crescent and Star: Turkey between Two Worlds*, New York: Farrar, Straus and Giroux, 2001, p. 62. The classic account of the making of the modern republic remains, despite the passage of more than four decades, Bernard Lewis, *The Emergence of Modern Turkey*, New York and Oxford: Oxford University Press, 1961.

4. Lewis, *The Emergence of Modern Turkey*, p. 125; for a detailed account of the Tanzimat, see pp. 73–125.

5. Interview with Halil Berktay, Istanbul, April 2002.

6. Lewis, *The Emergence of Modern Turkey*, p. 3.

7. Interview with Zeliha, Istanbul, April 2002.

8. Gareth Jenkins, *Political Islam in Turkey: Running West, Heading East?* New York and Basingstoke: Palgrave Macmillan, 2008, p. 111.

9. Ömer Taspinar, 'The Old Turks' Revolt', *Foreign Affairs*, November/December 2007.

10. Angel Rabasa and F. Stephen Larabee, *The Rise of Political Islam in Turkey*, Santa Monica: Rand, 2008, p. 37; www.rand.org/pubs/monographs/MG726.

11. For a portrait of Erbakan, see Stephen Kinzer, 'The Islamist Who Runs Turkey, Delicately', *New York Times*, 23 February 1997. In his book, published a few years later, Kinzer's judgement is somewhat harsher; see *Crescent and Star*, pp. 63–78.

12. Interview with Ali Bulaç, Istanbul, April 2002.

13. Visit to the War College, Istanbul, March 2002.
14. Visits to schools, Istanbul, March-April 2002.
15. More detail on the growth of *imam-hatip* schools can be found in Gareth Jenkins, *Political Islam in Turkey*, pp. 117, 128 and 159. By the mid-1990s, he reports, they had half a million students.
16. Senem Aydin and Rusen Çakir, *Political Islam in Turkey*, Brussels: Centre for European Policy Studies, 2007; www.ceps.eu.
17. Quoted in Aydin and Çakir, *Political Islam in Turkey*, p. 5.
18. Taspinar, 'The Old Turks' Revolt' (see note 9, above).
19. This account is based on a number of sources: Karl Vick, 'Al-Qaeda's Hand in Istanbul Plot', *Washington Post*, 13 February 2007; Gareth Jenkins, *Political Islam in Turkey*, pp. 205–10; Brian Glyn Williams and Feyza Altindag, 'El Kaide Turka: Tracing an Al-Qaeda Splinter Cell', *Terrorism Monitor*, 18 November 2004; and Soner Cagaptay and Emrullah Uslu, 'Hizballah in Turkey Revives: Al-Qaeda's Bridge between Europe and Iraq?' Washington Institute for Near East Policy, 25 January 2005. The extravagant figure of Louai Sakka is profiled in Karl Vick, 'A Bomb-Builder, "Out of the Shadows",' *Washington Post*, 20 February 2006.
20. Yigal Schleifer, 'Religious Kurds Become Key Vote in Turkey', *Christian Science Monitor*, 5 January 2009

CHAPTER 7: MUSLIM ARCHIPELAGO

1. Interview with 'Colonel Sam', Yala, southern Thailand, December 2004. This chapter draws on the BBC World Service radio series *Islam's Furthest Frontier* (2005). A useful short introduction to the role of Islam in the politics of the region is Greg Fealy, 'Islam in Southeast Asia: Domestic Pietism, Diplomacy and Security', in Mark Beeson (ed.), *Contemporary Southeast Asia: Regional Dynamics, National Differences*, New York and Basingstoke: Palgrave Macmillan, 2004.
2. Duncan McCargo, *Tearing Apart the Land: Islam and Legitimacy in Southern Thailand*, Ithaca: Cornell University Press, 2008, pp. 108 and 135ff.
3. Interviews in Tak Bai and nearby villages, December 2004. For accounts of the demonstration and its aftermath, see Andrew Per-

rin, 'Thailand's Bloody Monday', *Time*, 1 November 2004, and Duncan McCargo, *Tearing Apart the Land*, pp. 110–3.

4. McCargo, *Tearing Apart the Land*, pp. 183–8.

5. Public meeting in Kuala Lumpur, November 2004. For a lively account of the Mahathir era, see Ian Buruma, *God's Dust: A Modern Asian Journey*, New York: Farrar, Straus, Giroux, 1989.

6. Brian Lapping, *End of Empire*, London: Grenada, 1985, p. 154.

7. Interviews in Kuala Lumpur, November 2004. On the role of Anwar Ibrahim since leaving prison, see Ian Buruma, 'Letter from Malaysia', *New Yorker*, 18 May 2009.

8. Interviews at the trial of Abu Bakr Bashir, Jakarta, December 2004. (His name is often written Abu Bakar Ba'asyir, but I have preferred a simplified spelling which also reflects how the name is pronounced.)

9. Ruth McVey, 'Faith as the Outsider: Islam in Indonesian Politics', in James P. Piscatori (ed.), *Islam in the Political Process*, Cambridge: Cambridge University Press, 1983, p. 200–1.

10. Azyumardi Azra, Dina Afrianty, and Robert W. Hefner, 'Pesantren and Madrasa: Muslim Schools and National Ideals in Indonesia', in Robert W. Hefner and Muhammad Qasim Zaman (eds.), *Schooling Islam: The Culture and Politics of Modern Muslim Education*, Princeton: Princeton University Press, 2007.

11. The website, which has a small English section, is http://almukmin-ngruki.com. My visit to the school was in December 2004.

12. Lapping, *End of Empire*, pp. 18–9.

13. V. G. Kiernan, *The Lords of Human Kind: European Attitudes to the Outside World in the Imperial Age*, London: Penguin, 1972, p. 91.

14. M. C. Ricklefs, *A History of Modern Indonesia*, Stanford: Stanford University Press, 3rd edition, 2001, especially pp. 193–205.

15. Greg Fealy, 'Radical Islam in Indonesia: History, Ideology and Prospects', in Greg Fealy and Aldo Borgu, *Local Jihad: Radical Islam and Terrorism in Indonesia*, Barton: Australian Strategic Policy Institute, 2005, pp. 19–25; www.aspi.org.au.

16. Donald E. Weatherbee, 'Darul Islam', in John L. Esposito (ed.), *The Oxford Encyclopedia of the Modern Islamic World*, New York and Oxford: Oxford University Press, 1995.

17. Fealy, 'Radical Islam in Indonesia', p. 23.

18. Fealy, 'Radical Islam', pp. 25ff.

19. Sally Neighbour, *In the Shadow of Swords: On the Trail of Terrorism from Afghanistan to Australia*, Sydney: HarperCollins, 2005, p. 291. Also valuable is Peter Taylor's detailed reconstruction of the Bali bombings in the second of his three-part BBC television documentary series *The Third World War—al Qaeda*, broadcast on 10 February 2004. Thanks to Taylor, we even know the e-mail address Hambali was using at the time of the planned attacks in Singapore (bob_marley123@yahoo.com).

20. This account is based largely on Sally Neighbour, *In the Shadow of Swords*, and, for the aftermath of the bombings, Greg Fealy, 'Radical Islam in Indonesia'.

21. Interview with Sidney Jones of the International Crisis Group, Singapore, December 2004; and subsequent ICG reports on radical Islam in Indonesia. On the de-radicalisation programme, see Paul Watson, 'Indonesia Anti–Terrorism Chief Says Monitoring and Trust Are Key', *Los Angeles Times*, 15 March 2009.

22. Interview with General Almonte, Manila, December 2004.

23. José Almonte, *Toward One Southeast Asia*, Manila: Institute for Strategic and Development Studies, 2004, p. 229.

CHAPTER 8: THE BOMB IN THE TURBAN

1. The meeting was at Wilton Park, a conference centre which serves as an arm of the British Foreign Office, in May 2006. Under the rules of engagement, I can report what was said but not who said it. See 'Healing the Cartoon Row Wounds', BBC News Online, 11 May 2006. This chapter draws on the BBC World Service radio series *Europe's Angry Young Muslims* (2006).

2. Quoted in Senem Aydin and Rusen Çakir, *Political Islam in Turkey*, Brussels: Centre for European Policy Studies, 2007; www.ceps.eu.

3. The fullest and most revealing account of the cartoon affair is Jytte Klausen, *The Cartoons that Shook the World*, New Haven and London: Yale University Press, 2009.

4. See the thoughtful essay 'European Liberalism and "the Muslim Question",' in Bhikhu Parekh, *A New Politics of Identity: Political Principles for an Interdependent World*, Basingstoke: Palgrave Macmillan, 2008.

5. Philip Lewis, *Islamic Britain: Religion, Politics and Identity among British Muslims*, London: I. B. Tauris, 1994. Lewis views the British Muslim experience through a Bradford lens, and provides a dispassionate account of both the Honeyford and Rushdie controversies.

6. *Yorkshire Post*, 18 January 1989.

7. *The Independent*, 16 January 1989.

8. *The Independent*, 21 July 1989.

9. One of the most skilful attempts to tease out its meanings is that of an American anthropologist, John R. Bowen, *Why the French Don't Like Headscarves: Islam, the State, and Public Space*, Princeton: Princeton University Press, 2007.

10. Bowen, *Why the French*, pp. 242–9.

11. Ian Buruma, *Murder in Amsterdam*, London: Penguin, 2006.

12. Buruma, *Murder in Amsterdam*, pp. 189–90.

13. Interviews in Berlin, March 2007. This section draws on my article 'Can Germany Learn to Live with Islam?' BBC News Online, 29 March 2007; and for statistics and other background information on International Crisis Group, *Islam and Identity in Germany*, Brussels: March 2007; www.crisisgroup.org/home/index.cfm?id= 4693.

14. Simone Kaiser, Marcel Rosenbach and Holger Stark, 'How the CIA Helped Germany Foil Terror Plot', *Spiegel Online*, 10 September 2007.

15. Confidential British government report published by the *Sunday Times*, 30 May 2004.

16. See Alison Pargeter, *The New Frontiers of Jihad: Radical Islam in Europe*, London: I. B. Tauris, 2008; especially Chapter Two.

17. Daniel Benjamin and Steven Simon, *The Next Attack: The Failure of the War on Terror and a Strategy for Getting It Right*, New York: Times Books, 2005, p. 6.

18. Interviews in Leeds, January 2006.

19. For a portrait of Muhammad Siddique Khan, see Nasreen Suleaman, 'The Mystery of "Sid",' BBC News Online, 19 October 2005.

20. Sebastian Rotella, 'Dangerous, Endangered: A Look Inside Al Qaeda', *Los Angeles Times*, 2 April 2008.

21. Interviews in Paris, January 2006.

22. Interviews in The Hague, February 2006.
23. An influential example is Robert S. Leiken, 'Europe's Angry Muslims', *Foreign Affairs*, July/August 2005.
24. See, for example, Jytte Klausen, *The Islamic Challenge: Politics and Religion in Western Europe*, New York and Oxford: Oxford University Press, 2005; and Jonathan Laurence and Justin Vaisse, *Integrating Islam: Political and Religious Challenges in Contemporary France*, Washington, DC: Brookings Institution Press, 2006.

CHAPTER 9: HEARTS AND MINDS

1. Interview in Washington, DC, May 2005. Hoffman has since left Rand to become a professor at Georgetown University. Parts of this chapter were presented as a paper on 'The War of Ideas' at a workshop organised by the Royal United Services Institute (RUSI) on 'Intelligence and the Sociology of Terrorism' at St Antony's College, Oxford, 8–9 December 2006.
2. See Dave Moniz and Tom Squitieri, 'After Grim Rumsfeld Memo, White House Supports Him', *USA Today*, 22 October 2003; which includes a link to the text of the memo (dated 16 October).
3. For the mood of the moment, see Fareed Zakaria, 'Why Do They Hate Us?' *Newsweek*, 15 October 2001. 'The United States,' he concluded, writing in the white heat of 9/11, 'must help Islam enter the modern world.' For his more modest recommendations, almost eight years on, see 'Learning to Live with Radical Islam', *Newsweek*, 9 March 2009.
4. Seyyed Hossein Nasr, quoted in Stevenson Swanson, 'From Golden Age to an Embattled Faith', *Chicago Tribune*, 8 February 2004.
5. 'Cod Marxism', as it was memorably described to me at a conference in the Oxfordshire countryside, when I ventured to suggest that under-development might be part of the social backdrop, even if not the proximate cause of terrorism.
6. See Olivier Roy, *The Failure of Political Islam*, Cambridge, Mass.: Harvard University Press, 1994, and Ibrahim A. Karawan, *The Islamist Impasse*, Adelphi Paper 314, London: International Institute for Strategic Studies, 1997.

7. See Fawaz A. Gerges, *The Far Enemy: Why Jihad Went Global*, Cambridge: Cambridge University Press, 2005.

8. Bruce Riedel, *The Search for Al Qaeda: Its Leadership, Ideology, and Future*, Washington, DC: Brookings Institution Press, 2008, p. 33.

9. David Kilcullen, *The Accidental Guerrilla: Fighting Small Wars in the Midst of a Big One*, London: Hurst, 2009, pp. 286 and 300.

10. Mark Juergensmeyer, *Terror in the Mind of God*, Berkeley: University of California, 2001, p. 187. For the idea of violence as the flip-side of humiliation, I am indebted to Suroosh Irfani, whom I quote in Chapter Three.

11. Susan B. Glasser and Steve Coll, 'The Web as Weapon', *Washington Post*, 9 August 2005.

12. See, for example, a three-part series on the internet and the *jihad* in the *Washington Post*, 7–9 August 2005 (see note 11, above); and Bruce Hoffman, *The Use of the Internet by Islamic Extremists*, testimony presented to the House Permanent Select Committee on Intelligence, 4 May 2006; www.rand.org/pubs/testimonies/2006/RAND_CT262–1.pdf

13. A phrase used by Paul Eedle during a seminar at Birkbeck College, University of London, 5 February 2005. See also his 'Terrorism.com', *Guardian*, 17 July 2002, and his documentary *Jihad TV*, shown on Britain's Channel 4 on 6 November 2006.

14. The text of John Brennan's speech can be found at www.whitehouse.gov and a summary in Spencer S. Hsu and Joby Warrick, 'Obama's Battle Against Terrorism To Go Beyond Bombs and Bullets', *Washington Post*, 6 August 2009.

15. Stockholm conference, March 2008, organised by the Swedish National Defence College and the UK Defence Academy. See 'Grappling with Global Terror Conundrum', BBC News Online, 15 March 2008.

16. For a profile of Nagl, see Peter Maass, 'Professor Nagl's War', *New York Times*, 11 January 2004. In 2008 Nagl retired from the army and now heads a Washington think-tank.

17. Peter Maass, 'Professor Nagl's War'.

18. George Packer, 'Knowing the Enemy', *New Yorker*, 18 December 2006; a profile of Kilcullen. See also Kilcullen, *The Accidental Guerrilla*.

19. Marc Sageman, *Leaderless Jihad: Terror Networks in the Twenty-First Century*, Philadelphia: University of Pennsylvania Press, 2008, pp. 71–88.

20. Bruce Hoffman, 'Global Terrorist Threat: Is Al-Qaeda on the Run or on the March?' *Middle East Policy*, Summer 2007.

21. I've been unable to track down the date of the cartoon; and the cartoonist himself says he doesn't remember. See also Mahmood Mamdani, *Good Muslim, Bad Muslim: America, the Cold War, and the Roots of Terror*, New York: Pantheon, 2004.

22. John L. Esposito and Dalia Mogahed, *Who Speaks for Islam? What a Billion Muslims Really Think*, New York: Gallup Press, 2007. See also their article 'Battle for Muslims' Hearts and Minds: The Road Not (Yet) Taken', *Middle East Policy*, Spring 2007.

23. Tony Blair, speech to business leaders in Dubai, 20 December 2006; http://www.number10.gov.uk/Page10661

24. Douglas Hurd, speaking in an *Analysis* programme, 'Fear and Voting', BBC Radio 4, 22 April 2004.

25. Bruce Riedel, *The Search for Al Qaeda* (see note 8, above), p. 11.

26. Thomas Hegghammer, 'Jihadi Studies', *Times Literary Supplement*, 4 April 2008. See also his 'Osama bin Laden's True Priorities', www.guardian.co.uk, 3 December 2007.

ACKNOWLEDGEMENTS

My thanks are due, first, to the BBC World Service, which has employed me for more than twenty years as a Middle East and Islamic affairs analyst, and sent me at regular intervals to wander through the world of Islam. It has also allowed me to use BBC copyright material.

Much of the book was written while I was a visiting fellow at Princeton. I am grateful to Bernard Haykel and Joyce Slack—of the Transregional Institute for the Study of the Contemporary Middle East, North Africa and Central Asia—for their hospitality and for guiding a journalist through some of the mysteries of academic life. A number of Princeton colleagues read and commented on individual chapters—Muhammad Qasim Zaman, Miriam Künkler, Pascal Ménoret, Mike Laffan and Senem Aslan. In many cases they saved me from error; occasionally I have been rash enough not to heed their advice. My lively students, in a seminar course on young Muslims in Europe, gave me food for thought, not least on what makes the American melting-pot different from European multi–culturalism.

Three BBC producers have accompanied me on my travels and turned our journeys into radio programmes—Michael Gallagher, Bill Law and, especially, Zina Rohan, who also commented extensively on the manuscript. My Indonesian colleague Anton Alifandi kindly read the chapter on south-east Asia. The unsung heroes and heroines of every journalist's travels are the 'fixers' who translate, set up meetings, cut through red tape and generally make the difference between success and failure. I am indebted to them all.

ACKNOWLEDGEMENTS

Peter Unwin, author and former diplomat, read the manuscript and offered suggestions.

Michael Dwyer is the calmest and most helpful of publishers, and his support has been indispensable.

SELECT BIBLIOGRAPHY

A brief selection, from an enormous literature, for the general reader wanting to explore particular issues or countries in more detail.

Abrahamian, Ervand, *A History of Modern Iran*, Cambridge: Cambridge University Press, 2008.

Brown, L. Carl, *Religion and State: The Muslim Approach to Politics*, New York: Columbia University Press, 2000.

Buruma, Ian, *Murder in Amsterdam: Liberal Europe, Islam, and the Limits of Tolerance*, New York and London: Penguin, 2006.

Coll, Steve, *Ghost Wars: The Secret History of the CIA, Afghanistan and Bin Laden, from the Soviet Invasion to September 10, 2001*, New York and London: Penguin, 2005.

Devji, Faisal, *Landscapes of the Jihad: Militancy, Morality, Modernity*, London: Hurst, 2005.

Evans, Martin, and John Phillips, *Algeria: Anger of the Dispossessed*, New Haven and London: Yale University Press, 2007.

Esposito, John L. (ed.), *The Oxford Encyclopedia of the Modern Islamic World*, New York and Oxford: Oxford University Press, 2nd edition, 2009.

Esposito, John L., and John O. Voll (eds), *Makers of Contemporary Islam*, New York and Oxford: Oxford University Press, 2001.

Fuller, Graham, and Rend Rahim Francke, *The Arab Shi'a: The Forgotten Muslims*, London: Palgrave Macmillan, 2000.

Hourani, Albert, *A History of the Arab Peoples*, London: Faber & Faber, 1991.

Jenkins, Gareth, *Political Islam in Turkey: Running West, Heading East?* New York and Basingstoke: Palgrave Macmillan, 2008.

Kepel, Gilles, *Jihad: The Trail of Political Islam*, London: I. B. Tauris, 2002.

Klausen, Jytte, *The Islamic Challenge: Religion and Politics in Western Europe*, New York and Oxford: Oxford University Press, 2005.

Lapidus, Ira, *A History of Islamic Societies*, Cambridge: Cambridge University Press, 2nd edn 2002.

Lawrence, Bruce (ed.), *Messages to the World: The Statements of Osama bin Laden*, London and New York: Verso, 2005.

Lewis, Bernard, *The Emergence of Modern Turkey*, New York and Oxford: Oxford University Press, 1961.

Lia, Brynjar, *The Society of the Muslim Brothers in Egypt: The Rise of an Islamic Mass Movement 1928–1942*, Reading: Ithaca Press, 1998.

Mandaville, Peter, *Global Political Islam*, London and New York: Routledge, 2007

Mango, Andrew, *Atatürk*, London: John Murray, 1999.

Marsot, Afaf Lutfi al-Sayyid, *A Short History of Modern Egypt*, Cambridge: Cambridge University Press, 1985.

McCargo, Duncan, *Tearing Apart the Land: Islam and Legitimacy in Southern Thailand*, Ithaca: Cornell University Press, 2008.

Mottahedeh, Roy, *The Mantle of the Prophet: Religion and Politics in Iran*, New York and London: Penguin, 1987.

National Commission on Terrorist Attacks upon the United States, *The 9/11 Commission. Report*, New York: W. W. Norton, 2004 (available at www.9–11commission.gov)

Neighbour, Sally, *In the Shadow of Swords: On the Trail of Terrorism from Afghanistan to Australia*, Sydney: HarperCollins, 2005.

Ramadan, Tariq, *Western Muslims and the Future of Islam*, New York and Oxford: Oxford University Press, 2004.

Al-Rasheed, Madawi, *A History of Saudi Arabia*, Cambridge: Cambridge University Press, 2002.

Reidel, Bruce, *The Search for Al Qaeda: Its Leadership, Ideology, and Future*, Washington, DC: Brookings Institution Press, 2008.

Robinson, Francis (ed.), *The Cambridge Illustrated History of the Islamic World*, Cambridge: Cambridge University Press, 1996.

Roy, Olivier, *Globalised Islam: The Search for a New Umma*, London: Hurst, 2004.

Stern, Jessica, *Terror in the Name of God: Why Religious Militants Kill*, New York: HarperCollins, 2003.

Wright, Lawrence, *The Looming Tower: Al-Qaeda and the Road to 9/11*, London: Allen Lane, 2006.

GLOSSARY

alam	battle standard
aqidah	creed
Ashura	the tenth day of the month of Muharram (when the Shi'a commemorate the death of Hussein, grandson of the Prophet)
bid'a	innovation
dar al-islam	house (or realm) of Islam
da'wa	mission, proselytisation
faqih	jurist
fatwa	ruling (by a religious scholar)
fiqh	Islamic jurisprudence
fitna	discord, strife
hajj	pilgrimage to Mecca
hammam	Turkish bath
hijab	headscarf
hudud	prescribed punishments in Islamic law
husseiniyya	Shi'ite meeting-place
ijma	consensus
ijtihad	independent reasoning
imam	prayer leader
intifada	uprising
irfan	mystical knowledge
jahiliyya	ignorance; the pre-Islamic Dark Age
jihad	moral struggle, or holy war
madrasa	seminary
Mahdi	the 'awaited one', the Muslim messiah

majlis al-shura	consultative council
maslaha	the common good
mujahidin	warriors in a holy war
mustazafin	the dispossessed
mutawa	religious police
pesantren	Islamic boarding-school
salaf	ancestors; the first three generations of Muslims
sayyid	cleric who claims descent from the Prophet
Shi'ism	the 'partisans of Ali' (the main minority branch of Islam)
Shari'a	Islamic law
shirk	idolatry
Sufism	Islamic mysticism
Sunnism	the majority branch of Islam
takfir	excommunication
Tanzimat	19th-century Ottoman reforms
taqlid	imitation
tariqat	Sufi orders
tawhid	oneness of God; monotheism
ulama	religious scholars
umma	the worldwide community of Muslims
velayet-i–faqih	guardianship (or rule) of the jurist

INDEX